HITLER'S WAR
BENEATH THE WAVES

HITLER'S WAR
BENEATH THE WAVES

MICHAEL FITZGERALD

This edition published in 2020 by Arcturus Publishing Limited
26/27 Bickels Yard, 151–153 Bermondsey Street,
London SE1 3HA

AD006668UK

Printed in the UK

CONTENTS

INTRODUCTION

The conflict at sea during the Second World War was brutal and for six years crews of U-boats, merchant ships and warships engaged in a fierce battle. Britain was heavily dependent on imports and its merchant fleet was essential for its survival, so Germany's U-boats worked tirelessly to strangle its supplies at source. For two years Britain and its empire stood alone against the Germans and came close to defeat.

Hitler's War Beneath the Waves begins by examining the preparations for war made by the belligerent nations. All were capable of fighting a defensive war but none were equipped for a long battle of attrition.

The 'Phoney War', an eight-month period of military inactivity on the Western Front between September 1939 and May 1940, was not reflected at sea. U-boats attacked British shipping and inflicted heavy casualties. Even the naval base in Scapa Flow was penetrated by a lone submarine and the *Royal Oak* was destroyed in the harbour.

The organization of the naval war is described, including the intelligence battles, the development of more sophisticated technical systems, the introduction of convoys and the different submarine tactics of Britain, Germany and Italy. Living conditions on merchant ships and submarines are also examined.

The Battle of the Atlantic was the key focus of the war at sea. Dönitz devoted most of his efforts to that region and came close to choking off British imports, before the weight of numbers led to his defeat.

In the Mediterranean theatre Britain fought with Italy and Germany to hold on to Malta and North Africa and preserve

A triumphant return to the German naval base at Kiel for U-47, *a Type VIIB U-boat commanded by Günther Prien, after sinking the HMS* Royal Oak *at the Home Fleet Anchorage of Scapa Flow, 1939.*

control of the Suez Canal. Britain was in danger of losing this naval battle but eventually triumphed.

The Arctic convoys began in 1941 and for four years supplied the Soviet Union with aircraft, weapons and materials. After 1943 they were primarily continued for political rather than military reasons but during the dark years of 1941 to 1943 they were a vital lifeline. Without the essential supplies they took to Russia, Soviet resistance would have collapsed.

Africa and Asia also saw battles between U-boats and shipping, though these were on a smaller scale than the conflicts in the Atlantic, Mediterranean and Arctic.

The final defeat of the U-boats saw diminishing numbers of submarines fight on bravely against overwhelming odds. Most were destroyed at the end of the war.

Hitler's War Beneath the Waves concludes by recording the horrific casualties suffered by the crews of merchant ships and U-boats. In addition, the treatment of surrendered German submariners was often poor and it certainly violated the Geneva Convention.

U-boats and their crews were demonized in Allied propaganda as cruel, cowardly assassins. However, they were no more to be blamed than bombers flattening cities, tanks demolishing buildings or mines sinking ships or blowing up troops. In reality the crew members of the U-boats were brave men who, like their Allied counterparts, fought for their country and tried to achieve victory.

CHAPTER ONE

PREPARATIONS FOR WAR

The outbreak of war in 1939 found all of the major combatants unprepared. Under the terms of the Treaty of Versailles, the German army was limited to 100,000 men and its naval strength was restricted to a total of 15,000 men, six battleships, twelve destroyers, six cruisers and twelve torpedo boats. New boats were forbidden except as replacements for old vessels and these were limited to a size of 19,000 tons. Germany was forbidden to possess submarines or an air force.[1]

GERMAN RE-ARMAMENT

The Weimar Republic was as anxious as the Third Reich to evade the restrictions imposed upon it, so secret re-armament, often involving construction and testing in foreign countries, was carried out through dummy corporations. A torpedo research programme was developed in Sweden and although the navy was only allowed to build new ships as replacements for old vessels, they took care to make the new vessels as technically advanced as possible.

The German government began the clandestine development of new submarines in spite of the ban on their possession. It set up an office to examine wartime U-boats and advise on the types and numbers that were considered necessary. In 1922 an undertaking known as the IvS (*Ingenieurskantoor voor Scheepsbouw* – Engineering Office for Shipbuilding) was set up in Holland and it was speedily identified by Lieutenant Commander Wilhelm Canaris (later Admiral Canaris) as a suitable cover for designing and constructing submarines. Canaris suggested to Captain Walther Lohmann, technically head of the Sea Transport Division of the navy but in reality in charge of 'black' naval projects, that the Dutch office could be used to enable Germany to circumvent the Versailles ban on U-boats and other military activities.[2]

In charge of funds amounting to nearly $28 million, Lohmann subsidized the operation with an initial one million marks from the navy's secret budget. This was one of the many clandestine operations he financed over a period of four years for the German navy.

Lohmann also set up the Severa GmbH (*Seeflugzeug-Versuchsabteilung* – Seaplane Test Department) in collaboration with Lufthansa, in order to provide the basis of an illegal air arm for the navy. It created flying schools, aerodromes and bases where seaplanes and other aircraft were developed. The Japanese military attaché visited the German naval command in 1925 and observed that the construction of aeroplanes was in an advanced stage of development.

The IvS obtained an order in 1925 to build two submarines for the Turkish navy, which were constructed at the Rotterdam docks. Soon Spain, Argentina, Russia, Finland, Mexico and Japan approached the IvS and a number of submarines were built for foreign countries under its auspices.[3] At home some of the equipment necessary for submarines, such as radio equipment, underwater sound machinery, diesel engines and even periscopes, was manufactured by companies like Zeiss and Lorenz.[4]

By 1929 the German government felt confident enough to begin building surface ships of a larger size and a greater tonnage than permitted by the Treaty of Versailles. This open violation of its treaty obligations raised not the slightest protest from France or Britain.

Emboldened by this, the navy devised an ambitious re-armament plan known as *Umbau* (reconstruction), which was approved by the Weimar Defence Ministry in 1932. That year saw the first official training course for submariners who had previously trained in secret on vessels designed and constructed for foreign countries. It was presented to the world as an 'anti-submarine school' but hardly anyone believed this deception.[5]

Hitler's appointment as Chancellor in 1933 transformed the military situation in Germany. For the first two years he re-armed the German forces in secret and on a small scale. Hess declared that 'guns will make us powerful; butter will only make us fat' but until 1938 he consistently put butter before guns.[6] However, Hitler's strategic planning envisaged a wider war in 1942 or 1943 and he knew that every branch of the German military was incapable of a prolonged conflict.

In 1935 he signed the Anglo-German Naval Agreement and obtained surprisingly generous terms from the British. The treaty allowed Germany to build surface ships to a maximum of 35 per cent of British naval strength and no restrictions were placed on developing submarines. Following this agreement, Hitler pressed ahead with open re-armament. Every area of the military developed rapidly, including the navy. It remained the Cinderella of the armed forces, but for the first time in years it could look forward to a programme of expansion and development.[7]

The shortage of raw materials presented problems for Germany once it was at war. However, the extensive use of

A fleet of German submarines at Kiel in 1938 set out for inspection by Admiral Horthy, Regent of Hungary, who was the guest of Adolf Hitler.

ersatz (synthetic) products enabled the country to overcome these difficulties, until the plants manufacturing them were destroyed by bombing raids in 1944. In terms of the armaments available to the European powers in 1939, each country was capable of fighting a defensive war successfully or overcoming weaker nations. What Britain, France, Italy and Germany lacked was the military capacity to defeat one another. The French collapse in 1940 owed more to bad generalship, complacency and political weakness than to any military inferiority.

Another myth believed by all of the combatants was the statement in 1932 by Stanley Baldwin that 'the bomber will always get through'.[8] This mistaken idea led to the building of too many heavy bombers and insufficient fighter planes. Chamberlain's government, locked into this paradigm, estimated that London alone would suffer huge casualties from bombing during the first week of the war. Their figures were over-estimated to such an extent that they exceeded the total number of casualties suffered by the UK during the entire course of the war.[9]

The British and the French were as unprepared as the Germans for a major war, as both countries had been disarming for some years for different reasons. The British government's main domestic priority was reducing public expenditure while the French preferred to spend money on social projects. As a result, expenditure on defence was curtailed drastically. Inevitably that meant stretched resources when war broke out.

BRITISH RESOURCES

On paper, Britain was strong at the outbreak of war. The Royal Navy in 1939 was the largest and most powerful navy in the world. It possessed 15 battleships, 7 aircraft carriers, 68 cruisers, 184 destroyers, 48 escort and patrol vessels and 60 submarines. Numerically no nation could compete with its shipping.[10]

Another German submarine is launched to menace Allied shipping.

For all this strength in numbers, coupled with centuries of successful experience of naval warfare, there were hidden problems. The British were too complacent about the superiority of the Royal Navy. Many of its vessels were obsolescent and its attitude towards submarine warfare was antiquated. It attempted to model and construct its underwater fleet on the basis of surface vessels and favoured size over speed and performance.

The outbreak of the war saw the British Empire at the height of its power and territory. It could draw on resources from around the world but as a result it was forced to defend huge areas and the Royal Navy had to be active on four continents. However, the Treaty of Washington in 1923 restricted its growth by forbidding it to be larger than the United States navy. It was not until the war was already in progress that the Americans began to develop the largest navy in the world and were content to have the second largest fleet during the years of peace. By restricting the number of battleships Britain could build the Treaty hampered naval development.[11]

On the outbreak of war, the Royal Navy had a worldwide network of bases and arsenals and the fleet took the lion's share of the military budget. One of its strengths was that the old battlecruisers had been converted into aircraft carriers, so when war came Britain had more aircraft carriers than any other nation. They were the most advanced vessels of their type and the British Fleet Air Arm was the largest naval air force in the world.[12] Britain's possession of Gibraltar enabled it to guard the access from the Mediterranean to the Atlantic Ocean, while Alexandria controlled access to the Suez Canal. Malta was vital in terms of transporting supplies to Egypt and was under British control at the onset of the war.

More distant bases were Singapore and Hong Kong, Singapore being referred to as 'the Gibraltar of the Indian

Ocean'. India provided bases for the Navy and Australia, New Zealand and South Africa offered harbours and support. This widespread dispersion of the fleet had negative as well as positive consequences. The bulk of the available ships were focused on enemies in Asia or the Mediterranean rather than the Atlantic Ocean and this lack of sufficient ships in what became a crucial area in the war at sea cost Britain dearly.[13]

Nevertheless, British scientific and engineering ingenuity strengthened the Allied side. The new engineering department of the Royal Navy was created in 1937 and worked on developing radar and sonar systems for the fleet.[14]

All of these strengths were counterbalanced by significant weaknesses. The fall of Singapore and Hong Kong showed it was impossible for adequate defence to be provided so far from home bases and supply chains. Strength in numbers was not enough to overcome the problems of over-extended lines of supply and communication.

Further complacency was shown by the mistaken belief that the ASDIC (Allied Submarine Detection Investigation Committee) system was a foolproof method of detecting submarines before they were able to attack. The reality was that ASDIC was limited in its range of operation and was incapable of detecting a U-boat on the surface. As the Germans had been practising submarine manoeuvres on the surface and at night with the intention of making them their principal form of attack the ASDIC system was largely ineffective.[15]

ASDIC was devised in 1917 by the committee which gave its name to the system. It pulsed a series of ultrasonic waves which were beamed underwater in the shape of a cone. The sound echoes from an enemy vessel were reflected back to the ship and the time between their transmission and reception was used to determine the range. This could determine the position of submarines up to a mile distant but it could not reveal depth beneath the water. Even so, ASDIC was fitted to ships' hulls and was believed to be a complete defence against submarines.[16]

The truth was that ASDIC was not only useless against a night attack or a U-boat on the surface but it was also unreliable in stormy seas. When ASDIC was used during the Second World War a further limitation was revealed. A ship had to release its depth charges immediately above the U-boat but this required the vessel to travel so slowly that it risked disabling its electronic systems. ASDIC had no margin for error and a ship attacking a submarine ran the risk of the underwater explosion caused by the depth charges sinking the attacking vessel.[17]

Britain's reliance on imports of food and raw materials made it vulnerable to maritime attack and the disruption of its supply lines by U-boats almost forced it to surrender in 1917. This experience should have led to a recognition of the dangers of submarine warfare and the need to protect supplies at all costs. Instead, a complacent belief that ASDIC could deal with the U-boats meant no adequate preparations were made.[18]

One area where British forward planning was successful was the realization of the importance of air cover for shipping. RAF Coastal Command was active from the beginning of the war in protecting vessels and this made a huge difference to preventing losses and identifying and eliminating German raiders.[19] On the other hand, Dönitz had no aerial cover for his submarines and German surface ships were virtually unprotected by aircraft outside the Baltic Sea region. In spite of the demands by the navy for air support Göring refused to concede any planes to assist them and it was not until 1942 that Hitler overruled him and allowed aerial cover. By then it was too late to affect the outcome of the war.[20]

FRENCH RESOURCES

British complacency and old-fashioned naval thinking created problems for both the Royal and the Merchant Navy but French attitudes were even more disastrous. With the fourth largest navy in the world France should have been able to muster an effective fighting force but it did nothing of the kind. France's military planning focused on a land war supported by heavy bombers and hardly any thought was given to its powerful navy.

The French fleet was principally designed to be active in the Mediterranean. But when the war against Germany came, geography hindered the navy from taking an active part and the French surrender meant that its naval forces became a problem rather than an asset.[21] In 1931 the French built the *Surcouf*, named after a 19th-century pirate. It was the largest submarine in the world but, as with the Royal Navy, the obsession with size reduced its effectiveness. The submarine could only submerge slowly and the vessel's guns were lodged in an area that made them vulnerable. Heavy and slow, it constantly suffered from mechanical problems and was almost useless as a weapon of war. Eventually it was sunk during the conflict in mysterious circumstances.[22]

At the beginning of the war 40 per cent of the French fleet was at Toulon, 40 per cent was in French North Africa and the remaining 20 per cent was dispersed between Alexandria, the French West Indies and Britain. As a result of this disposition the fleet saw almost no action during the 'Battle of France'. The French navy should have been better prepared for a war against Germany and could have used its ships to restrict German naval activity, but the alliance with Britain meant that the French fleet was largely focused on the perceived threat from Italy. It was left to the Royal Navy to guard the Channel and the North Sea.[23]

GERMAN RESOURCES

The Germans began limited naval expansion before Hitler became Chancellor. He took little interest in naval matters, but his determination to upgrade and expand every aspect of German military capacity allowed Admiral Erich Raeder, head of the navy, to win his approval for an ambitious building programme. Raeder wanted a large fleet of heavy cruisers, destroyers, torpedo boats, minesweepers, auxiliary cruisers and submarines. His intention was to match the Royal Navy in terms of size and number of ships and he consistently resisted Dönitz's pleas for more U-boats rather than surface vessels.[24] Raeder had failed to grasp the importance of submarines in naval warfare. The admiral then tried to persuade Hitler that the German navy could be the key to strengthening the nation in war, but the Chancellor preferred to give funding to Göring's Luftwaffe instead. The idea of heavy bombers obsessed him, whereas he had no understanding of the importance of sea power.[25]

PLAN Z

In early 1939 Raeder won Hitler's approval for an ambitious programme of naval expansion known as Plan Z. This was scheduled for completion in 1948 and focused on surface ships. The belief of its advocates was that the key to winning a naval war against Britain was by constructing fast, heavily armed cruisers supported by a fleet of aircraft carriers. The Germans were as mistaken as the British in believing that ASDIC was a foolproof detection system which would make any significant use of submarines in naval warfare futile. This attitude, along with Hitler's obsessional preference for size, enabled Raeder to dismiss Dönitz's advocacy of a large fleet of U-boats as the key to winning a naval war.[26]

Admiral Erich Raeder was set in his ways and failed to grasp the importance of submarines in modern naval warfare.

The navy saw active service during the Spanish Civil War. Franco's rebels were backed by Italy and Germany and on the outbreak of war several ships were sent to Spain. In July 1936, the heavy cruisers *Deutschland* and *Admiral Scheer* and the light cruiser *Köln* were sent to assist the rebels, along with the 2nd Torpedo Boat flotilla.[27] The first action of the *Deutschland* was not military but humanitarian. It evacuated 9,300 refugees, which included 4,550 Germans. Later the *Deutschland* and the *Admiral Graf Spee* were put in charge of an arms embargo and were asked to patrol the region between Cabo de Gata and Cabo de Oropesa. On 29 May 1937 the *Deutschland* was attacked by two Spanish government bombers and 31 people were killed and 110 wounded. The *Admiral Scheer* responded to this attack by shelling Almeria on 31 May, killing 20 civilians and wounding 50 more. The Republicans then sent submarines to attack the German ship *Leipzig* near the port of Oran between 15 and 18 June 1937 and after this attack Germany withdrew its vessels from patrol duty.[28]

Eight U-boats then engaged in covert offensive action against Spanish government ships. However, Germany's naval contribution to Franco's campaign was small and its most effective fighting arm was the Luftwaffe, which notoriously bombed Guernica. The bulk of foreign military aid for Franco came from Mussolini, with 58 submarines, the Italian air force and ground troops.

By the time war broke out, little work had been carried out on the large fleet of new surface ships and with changed military priorities the navy was forced to abandon the programme. Only those ships commissioned before the war were completed. The battleships *Scharnhorst* and *Gneisenau* were built and the *Bismarck* and the *Tirpitz* were added to the fleet, along with the heavy cruisers *Blücher*, *Prinz Eugen*, *Deutschland* and *Graf Spee*.[29]

Raeder's plan was to use long-range cruisers to attack British ships, with U-boats playing a purely auxiliary function. He believed this would overcome British naval dominance and allow a small number of German battleships to play a decisive role in North Sea operations. The core of the plan was the building of ten battleships and four aircraft carriers, together with a large number of cruisers. Only a small force of U-boats was envisaged, in spite of attempts by Dönitz to build much larger numbers of submarines.

The amount of construction involved in Plan Z and the level of expenditure that would have been needed to bring it to fruition has led to it being regarded as a fantasy. Overall the project demanded more fuel, raw materials and other resources than Germany possessed or was capable of furnishing and it would have forced the national debt to soar to unprecedented levels. If it had genuinely been intended purely as a defensive programme these criticisms might be justified, but while not favouring a conflict on the scale of the First World War Raeder knew that a series of limited wars would allow Germany to exploit the resources of conquered nations. Plan Z would only have been realistic if it had been envisaged as a consequence of successful military action.

As with the naval plans of all the combatants, Plan Z and the existing naval programme for Germany emphasized surface ships rather than submarines. This imbalance of focus and development had a significant impact on the course of the war. The Plan Z programme led to the building of four ships costing 800 million Reichsmarks altogether, but for the same amount of money 100 U-boats could have been laid down, which would have had a greater effect on German naval capability.[30]

NAVAL INTELLIGENCE

German naval intelligence was the most efficient and sophisticated part of the Nazi intelligence services. Headed by the enigmatic Admiral Canaris, it appeared to be staffed almost exclusively by opponents of Hitler, including Canaris himself. His deputy Hans Oster became one of the key players in the German Resistance and was involved in the plot to assassinate Hitler in 1944, something he and Canaris had discussed since 1938. In spite of their hostility to their nation's leader, however, they remained committed to their country and succeeded in breaking the British naval code, which gave the Germans a huge intelligence advantage at the beginning of the war.

This achievement was the work of the *B-Dienst* (*Beobachtungsdienst* – observation service) section of German naval intelligence. The British success in cracking Enigma two years later is well known but the fact that the Germans cracked the British naval code is less generally realized. As early as 1939 German codebreakers were able to decipher encoded British messages and could read 50 per cent of naval traffic. This enabled them to plot the course and position of British ships and make the necessary preparations to attack them. Their foreknowledge of naval and merchant ship manoeuvres had a significant impact on the course of the naval war and was responsible for numerous unnecessary casualties.[31]

CHANGING APPROACH TO U-BOAT OPERATION

From 1934 onwards the engineer Hellmuth Walter worked for the German navy on developing a submarine capable of high speeds underwater. He did not complete his prototype until 1940, when he unveiled the V80 in Danzig. It was a small boat in the shape of a fish and it weighed 80 tons. In test voyages it achieved a speed of 28 knots (32 mph) underwater. Attempts to create larger vessels experienced technical problems and the project was never realized successfully.[32]

In 1935 Dönitz wrote a paper outlining his view of the proper use of U-boats in the event of a war with France or Russia. One of his observations was that:

> *In a war against an enemy who is not dependent on overseas supplies as a vital necessity, the task of our U-boats, in contrast to the World War, will not be the trade war, for which the U-boat in consequence of its low speed is little suited. The U-boat will be placed in a stationary position as close as possible before the enemy harbouring at the focal point of traffic. Attack target, the enemy warships and troop transports.[33]*

This was the established view of submarine warfare at that time and the same position was taken by the British, American, French, Italian and Japanese navies. It was also expected that the main European theatre of U-boat operations would be in the Mediterranean rather than the Atlantic. Both of these presuppositions proved to be mistaken.

Within a year of taking over Germany's submarine fleet, Dönitz turned his flotilla into a state of readiness for war. He made his crews carry out eight underwater exercises by day and six surface attacks by night, for five days a week. The combination of practical experience and the re-evaluation of existing theories on submarine warfare led him to adopt a completely different approach to U-boat operation.

Dönitz then evolved the *Rüdeltaktik* (wolfpack) method of attack, which was an idea he had first discussed during the First World War and some elements of the navy had come to favour. He came to see it as the most effective way of deploying his small U-boat fleet. His plans were based on the idea of a conflict against Russia, with the Baltic Sea being the main focus of operations, or against France, in which case he saw the Mediterranean as the principal battleground.[34]

CAMPAIGN PLANS

In 1936 Dönitz and the navy had their first major disagreement over procurement. Dönitz demanded a large number of small U-boats but the admirals preferred a smaller force of four-gun cruiser submarines. It was two years before the grandiose projects favoured by the navy were abandoned as unrealistic and during that time none of the small U-boats Dönitz wanted were built. This two-year moratorium meant that fewer submarines were available to Germany when war broke out.

In 1937 Hitler realized that war with Britain was a possibility and ordered the navy to draw up campaign plans. Raeder and Dönitz clashed over strategy and tactics with Raeder demanding huge warships and Dönitz a large fleet of submarines. By now Dönitz believed that attacking merchant shipping rather than the Royal Navy offered the best chance of success in a naval war, but his views were rejected.[35]

The prospect of war loomed large in 1938 and Dönitz intensified his preparations. In 1939 he conducted an exercise that convinced him that he needed 300 U-boats to win the naval war and that the main focus of their operations should be in the Atlantic rather than the Baltic or Mediterranean.

The strength of the German U-boat fleet at the outbreak of war was a mere 62 vessels, of which only ten were ready for action. There is no doubt that a large number of small submarines would have enabled the U-boat campaign to be more successful, but German preparations for war were as inadequate and outdated as those of Britain and France.

Admiral Karl Dönitz evolved the 'wolfpack' method of attack which was to be used so successfully by U-boats.

One of the fundamental problems for the German war effort was the absence of a properly co-ordinated central authority. There were no German equivalents to the Joint Chiefs of Staff and Hitler and Göring issued orders that the armed forces were expected to implement.[36]

This lack of central planning affected the navy less than the other services because neither Hitler nor Göring took much interest in naval matters. Raeder had a free hand to deploy his surface vessels and Dönitz was able to organize his submarines without undue interference.

The downside of Hitler's lack of interest in the navy was that it remained underfunded and neglected. Until the outbreak of war its role was seen as purely defensive, its only purpose being to guard the German coast and control the Baltic Sea.

Germany had nothing resembling the naval tradition of Britain but an attempt was made to popularize the navy among the people, through the use of 'sea-sport schools'. These were conducted on a lake near Berlin, where boys from across Germany received a short course in naval training. The school itself nestled in a pine forest south of Berlin.[37]

The Navy League had over 50,000 members. It developed a sense of pride in the German navy and awoke a more general interest in the sea among ordinary people.[38]

The war saw considerable conflict on the high seas and Germany's most effective weapon was its submarine fleet. The term U-boat is an English translation of the German word *Unterseeboot* – underwater boat. U-boat crews were highly trained and considered themselves an elite among German naval forces. Many were so proud of their service that at the end of the war they preferred to scuttle their boats rather than surrender.

U-BOAT READINESS

In spite of the inadequate number of U-boats available to the Germans before and at the beginning of the war, their superb quality, the outstanding training of the crews and the careful planning that Dönitz devoted to making them the most feared of all Nazi weapons of war, except for the V-missiles, meant that they were the readiest of all the armed forces of the Third Reich when war finally arrived.

Dönitz expressed his frank and radical views on submarine warfare in a book published in 1939 called *Bericht über FdU Kriegsspiel* (Report on the FdU War Game).[39] In the book he declared that 'the destruction of enemy trade' and attacking 'enemy sea communications' were 'the proper purpose of sea warfare'. He announced that he had trained his crews to attack on the surface and at night.

The British demonstrated their complacency by not reading Dönitz's book until 1942. Had they read it on its publication, they might have been better prepared for the wolfpack onslaught by submarines that devastated their ships for the first four years of the war.

In many respects Dönitz was ahead of his time in grasping the role of submarines in war, but his obstinacy and dogmatism were serious weaknesses. Autumn 1938 saw a series of manoeuvres in which U-boats carried out mock attacks on the surface. The successful exercise delighted Dönitz, but a young officer warned the admiral that the development of radar might make surface attacks by U-boats difficult. The Germans were testing a radar prototype at the time and had successfully detected objects much smaller than a submarine. However, Dönitz and the other naval officers refused to consider the possibility that radar might make their task impossible.[40]

Further problems were demonstrated during an exercise in the spring of 1939. Dönitz sent 15 U-boats in groups of four to attack a convoy of two ships and an escorting vessel. The submarines signalled to one another and surrounded the ships and on the basis of this unrealistic war game he declared: 'The simple principle of fighting a convoy of several steamers with several U-boats is correct. The convoy would have been destroyed.'

Once more, objections were raised to this complacent opinion but were summarily dismissed. The principal argument against assuming success was that there had been considerable signalling during the mock attacks, which in a real combat situation risked exposing the U-boats to danger.[41]

Dönitz dismissed the idea that U-boats alone could not destroy convoys in sufficient numbers and that air support was essential to success. Until war broke out, he believed that aircraft would play only a marginal role in the ocean conflict. But the reality of war soon made him recognize that aircraft played a pivotal role in supporting submarines.

BRITISH APPROACH TO SUBMARINE WARFARE

The Royal Navy's approach to submarine warfare and naval conflict in general was unrealistic throughout the inter-war years. They built a number of new submarines which continued the obsession with size over performance and suffered from numerous technical defects, in particular a tendency to leak oil. Unreliable torpedoes which could not be serviced or reloaded at sea added to the design faults. The submarines lacked range, speed and sufficient armament to be effective.[42]

These technical problems and poor design features were compounded by an unrealistic view of the role and capabilities of submarines. Night attacks on the surface were never practised and in daylight exercises torpedoes were principally discharged in single shots, rather than concentrated salvoes. The obsession with ASDIC meant that the ability of German hydrophones to detect British submarines was overlooked and only bitter first-hand experience of combat alerted their crews to the need for silence at sea.[43] Torpedo control and gun firing were primitive. The periscopes of British submarines were vastly inferior to their German counterparts and the same was true of their guidance systems.[44]

Some junior officers suggested adopting more flexible tactics and practising night attacks but their advice was ignored, as were repeated requests for air cover. Blinded by their notion of the infallibility of ASDIC, the Admiralty claimed that the system had 'virtually extinguished the submarine menace'. As a result, the protection of merchant ships was given a low priority and the convoy system was regarded as unnecessary. It is difficult not to agree with the assessment of Vice-Admiral Sir Peter Gretton, who wrote: 'We [the British] were criminally unprepared for the Battle of the Atlantic in 1939.'[45]

More long-term political and strategic errors also played their part. Until 1938 British naval planning was dominated by the prospect of war with Japan and little thought was given to the dangers posed by Germany or its fleet of U-boats.[46]

EVALUATION

As the crisis over Poland loomed in the summer of 1939, Hitler gave an incisive analysis of why he did not fear war with Britain and France. He believed both countries had poor leadership and that the war of 1914–18 had fatally weakened Britain, which meant that both countries were incapable of aggressive military action or assisting Poland. The French would not attack by land and if the British instituted a naval blockade he was unconcerned. Germany had sufficient stocks of food and raw materials and the Nazi–Soviet pact meant that the Germans would receive 'grain, cattle, coal, lead and zinc' from their new Russian allies.

Hitler was correct about the inability of Britain and France to wage an aggressive war. It was true that the First World War had nearly bankrupted Britain and though it still held its large empire the strain was becoming more pronounced as the recession continued to bite. And Stalin assisted the Germans with large quantities of essential raw materials up to the moment of invasion. The British and French were not in a position to afford assistance to Poland in spite of their declaration of war. On the other hand, Germany was not capable of defeating Britain and but for fundamental blunders by the French generals it should not have been able to beat France either. The reality in 1939 from a military point of view was that the two opposing forces were evenly balanced and neither side was capable of delivering a knockout blow to the other.

Dönitz felt that in spite of his limited resources a submarine campaign against merchant shipping was capable of bringing Britain to its knees. Germany had too few surface ships to compete with the Royal Navy and the U-boats at its disposal were better equipped to sink merchant shipping than take on destroyers and battleships.

None of the combatant nations were ready for a long war, but the Germans were in a better position to use their limited resources than the British and the French. The Allied navies were unprepared to deal with the unexpected assault by sea and their armies were not ready to face the blitzkrieg on land. In addition, the British remained fixated on the mirage of the impregnable nature of ASDIC and the power of their navy to contain any threat from submarines or surface ships. From the point of war at sea Dönitz was the only senior naval commander on either side with a coherent and realistic strategy.

The British and German preparations for war at sea were inadequate and mistaken but at least they both had plans. The French on the other hand had no serious naval strategy and the Italians had no desire to fight at all. Mussolini was aware of his country's weakness and only reluctantly joined the conflict when he mistakenly believed that the war in the West was all but over.

The Italian navy was large but badly handled and it proved no match for the British in the Mediterranean. Mussolini had never planned for a major war and this lack of preparedness became apparent once Italy began hostilities.

The United States remained outside the conflict, at least technically, until December 1941. Its navy was second only to Britain's in size and in some respects it was superior in quality. The primary focus of the US navy was on the perceived possibility of war with Japan, however, and militarily it was not prepared for a long conflict, in spite of its vast natural resources and large industrial capacity. American forces and officers had extremely limited experience of combat and in terms of war at sea their focus remained as fixed on the idea of large-scale battles between surface fleets as their European counterparts. There was little understanding of the idea of submarines being more than a purely auxiliary weapon.

All of the combatants entered the war – Britain, France and Germany in 1939, Italy in 1940 and Russia, Japan and America in 1941 – profoundly unprepared for a sustained conflict. All were capable of short campaigns but none had made serious plans for a long war. This lack of preparedness was to have severe consequences for all sides.[47]

NOTES

1 https://net.lib.byu.edu/~rdh7/wwi/versa/versa4.html/ (The terms of the Treaty of Versailles relating to Germany's naval, submarine and air force capabilities.)

2 F.L. Carsten, *The Reichswehr and the Generals, 1918–1933*, Oxford University Press, 1966

3 Ibid.

4 Ibid.

5 Ibid.

6 Burton H. Klein, *Germany's Economic Preparations for War*, Harvard University Press, 1968

7 Joseph Maiolo, *The Royal Navy and Nazi Germany, 1933–39: A Study in Appeasement and the Origins of the Second World War*, Macmillan, 1998

8 Keith Middlemas and John Barnes, *Baldwin*, Littlehampton Book Services, 1969

9 David Dutton, *Neville Chamberlain*, Arnold, 2001

10 https://ww2-weapons.com/fleets-1939/

11 Robert Gordon Kaufman, *Arms Control During the Pre-Nuclear Era: The United States and Naval Limitation Between the Two World Wars*, Columbia University Press, 1990

12 Kev Darling, *Fleet Air Arm Carrier War: The History of British Naval Aviation*, Pen and Sword, 2009

13 Dr Graham Watson, *Organisation of the Royal Navy 1939–1945*, http://www.naval-history.net/xGW-RNOrganisation1939-45.htm/

14 Jonathan Dimbleby, *The Battle of the Atlantic: How the Allies Won the War*, Penguin, 2015

15 David K. Brown, *Atlantic Escorts: Ships, Weapons and Tactics in World War II*, Naval Institute Press, 2007

16 Peter Padfield, *War Beneath the Sea: Submarine Conflict During World War II*, Wiley, 1998

17 Padfield, *War Beneath the Sea*

18 Ibid.

19 Dimbleby, op. cit.

20 Ibid.

21 Ibid.

22 J. Rusbridger, *Who Sank* Surcouf? *The Truth About the Disappearance of the Pride of the French Navy*, Century, 1991

23 Dimbleby, op. cit.

24 Padfield, *War Beneath the Sea*

25 Ibid.

26 Erich Gröner, *German Warships: 1815–1945*, Naval Institute Press, 1990

27 Antony Beevor, *The Battle for Spain: The Spanish Civil War 1936—1939*, Phoenix, 2006

28 Ibid.

29 Ibid.

30 Padfield, *War Beneath the Sea*

31 Jak P. Mallmann Showell, *German Naval Codebreakers*, Naval Institute Press, 2003

32 Jak P. Mallmann Showell, *The German Navy Handbook 1939–1945*, Sutton Publishing, 1999

33 Kap. z. S. K. Dönitz, 'Organisation der U-Bootswaffe,' 1935, quoted in Padfield, *War Beneath the Sea*

34 Karl Dönitz, *Memoirs: Ten Years and Twenty Days*, Frontline Books, 2012

35 Peter Padfield, *Dönitz: The Last Führer*, Victor Gollancz, 1993

36 Richard J. Evans, *The Third Reich in Power*, Penguin, 2005

37 Stephen Roberts, *The House that Hitler Built*, Methuen, 1937

38 Ibid.

39 Kap. z. S. K. Dönitz, *Bericht über FdU Kriegsspiel*, 1939. Quoted in Padfield, *Dönitz*

40 Padfield, *War Beneath the Sea*

41 Ibid.

42 Ibid.

43 Ibid.

44 William King, *The Stick and the Stars*, Hutchinson, 1958

45 Peter Gretton, review of Lord Hill-Norton, *Sea Power*, Faber and Faber, 1982

46 Paul M. Kennedy, *The Rise and Fall of British Naval Mastery*, Allen Lane, 1976

47 Padfield, *War Beneath the Sea*

CHAPTER TWO

EARLY SKIRMISHES

The first casualty of the naval war was the passenger liner *Athenia*, which was torpedoed 250 miles (400 km) north-west of Ireland on 3 September 1939. Under the rules of war this attack was illegal. Not only that but Dönitz had issued orders to his U-boat crews on the outbreak of war that they could attack merchant shipping in accordance with the established 'prize rules', but passenger ships were off limits. (Prize Regulations required submarine commanders to stop and search merchant vessels and then ensure that their crews were in a place of safety before they sank them.)

THE SINKING OF THE *ATHENIA*

The commander of *U-30* received this order and was sailing in the Atlantic when he saw smoke to the east. He piloted his submarine towards the smoke until he saw the masts of the steamer through the waves. The ship appeared to be heading directly towards his vessel.

After ordering the submarine to be readied for action, the commander observed the approaching ship through his periscope. Its funnel was pouring out smoke and it was still steering a course towards him. No other ships were in sight and he evaluated the situation.

U-30 was 1,000 yards (914 m) from the *Athenia* when its commander gave the order to fire the torpedoes. No one on the ship had seen the periscope rising through the water and nor did they see the approaching missile. Two salvoes were aimed at the ship but the second torpedo became stuck in the firing tube. This did not matter, because the first torpedo had struck the *Athenia* near the engine room. The force of the explosion plunged the ship into darkness and the waves came rushing over the deck.

The stricken *Athenia* began tilting towards port and the captain gave the order to abandon ship. As the process of marshalling the lifeboats began, people on the port side of the vessel saw the U-boat training its deck gun on the ship. Two shots were fired before the submarine dipped beneath the waves and disappeared.

Before the U-boat submerged, its commander realized his error of judgement. The sight of women and children on the deck of the *Athenia* filled him with horror as it dawned on him that he had sunk a passenger liner and not an armed merchant ship.[1]

Out of the 1,418 passengers and crew on the *Athenia*, 118 died. It was a public relations disaster for Germany and the episode was immediately compared to the sinking of the *Lusitania* in 1915. This is an anonymous survivor's account of the sinking of the *Athenia*.

> *I hadn't undressed when a clash like iron coming together and a great noise and jolt and then a deep boom and crash and then the lights flickered out – then I knew what had happened and jerked up quick and made for the door. I managed to find my way up and, just after, two women came along and their faces were as black as chimney sweeps. I saw*

three men dead and lying in the deck chairs from
concussion and the guns fired across the ship, and
some screamed when they saw them. For a moment
I saw a piece of rag lying a little way across, and I
went and picked it up and covered the face of one
that was dead, and then I saw a woman floating in
the sea and they flung her a spar, and just then a
young man got on the rail and jumped over. I felt
the water coming in before I got up, and a lady
who shared my cabin tried to go down to get her
money and couldn't for the water, so I only got up
in time. We were several hours in the lifeboat and it
was awful. Finally we got to the Knute Nelson and
it nearly swamped us and much shouting went on.
Finally they got a little more order.[2]

The Germans hastily disowned the sinking, suggesting that the
U-boat commander might have mistaken the ship for an armed
merchant vessel. It is strange that the *Athenia* was steering a
course directly towards the U-boat and though the captain
knew that war had begun he did not set out watches to look for
the presence of submarines. The likelihood is that he assumed
that as the captain of a passenger liner he had no need to be
concerned about enemy U-boats.

The submarine crew told the German authorities they
thought the *Athenia* was a troopship. But the most plausible
explanation is that news of the declaration of war made the
commander nervous and the sight of the *Athenia* sailing
directly towards his U-boat led him to assume he was under
attack. This was an understandable error of judgement, but the
sinking caused the U-boat campaign, at least temporarily, to be
conducted in a cautious manner.

THE SINKING OF THE *ROYAL OAK* IN SCAPA FLOW

Dönitz was heavily criticized for this tragedy, including by Hitler, who rebuked him for the commander's misjudgement, so he needed a spectacular success to redeem his tarnished reputation. The admiral then summoned one of his best U-boat captains.

Günther Prien was a fanatical Nazi and when Dönitz asked him to strike a blow at the heart of Britain he gladly accepted the challenge. Following Dönitz's instructions, Prien sailed for the British Naval Base at Scapa Flow in the Orkney Islands. Scapa Flow was considered impregnable and the British had created barriers to entry that made it impossible for any surface ship to penetrate.

However, the superficially imposing defences at Scapa Flow had not been maintained and the steel netting that formed part of the barrier had rusted away. On his appointment as First Lord of the Admiralty in September 1939, Churchill queried if the base was safely defended but was reassured that it remained impossible to penetrate.

Admiral Sir William French was less sanguine. He agreed that it was impossible for surface ships to break through the cordon, but suggested that a submarine could navigate its way through the open channel at Scapa Flow. His warnings fell on deaf ears and the Admiralty remained convinced that the base was impenetrable. They were certain the Germans had no idea of the poor state of the defences at Scapa Flow.

This complacent attitude was brutally shattered when in August 1939 Captain Horst Karle was sent to the Orkneys on a reconnaissance mission by naval intelligence. He took back a detailed survey of the badly maintained defences at Scapa Flow and his information was quickly forwarded to Dönitz. On 1 October 1939 he summoned Prien to meet him and asked him to evaluate the feasibility of the mission.

Lieutenant Captain Prien, fanatical Nazi and commander of the U-boat that sank the Royal Oak *in Scapa Flow. In all, he was credited with sinking more than 30 Allied ships during the war, totalling about 200,000 gross register tons (GRT).*

Prien, in his own words, 'worked through the whole thing like a mathematical problem' and the next day he returned to Dönitz and accepted the mission to attack Scapa Flow. The British had sunk blockships in the Kirk Sound channel to close the entrance, but Prien's submarine penetrated it and arrived within the base on 14 October. When he first surveyed the site there was no sign of any ships, but then he changed course and saw two vessels in the base, lying at anchor. One was the *Royal Oak* battleship. Prien readied his torpedoes and fired three salvoes at the ship. The first torpedo hit it and damaged it slightly while the second round fell wide, but the third round was the killer blow. The stricken ship exploded and began sinking rapidly and 833 out of the crew of 1,146 on the *Royal Oak* were killed by this torpedo attack. Prien made his way home with a sense of satisfaction, having destroyed a British battleship in its base in less than 15 minutes. It was a catastrophic demonstration of British complacency and lack of preparation for war.

On his return to Germany Prien was feted and the exultant Germans held a press conference. The impression received by foreign journalists was that the British had been criminally negligent, while others suggested that a spy must have provided the submarine commander with the necessary information. But the reality was that Karle's painstaking pre-war reconnaissance had enabled the Germans to identify the weak spots in Scapa Flow and plan the attack. The defensive precautions at the base were inadequate and following this fiasco they were drastically improved.

Scapegoats were found and French was dismissed, in spite of having been the man who warned of the poor state of the defences, along with the head of MI5, who was blamed for failing to detect the 'German spy' who, in the view of the British authorities, must have assisted the U-boats to find their quarry.

As well as scapegoating people who were not to blame, much time was wasted on a fruitless search for a non-existent German spy in the area. The truth was that patient and careful German reconnaissance and British complacency were responsible for the disaster.[3]

THE SINKING OF THE *BOSNIA*

The first merchant ship sunk by a U-boat was the *Bosnia*, on 5 September 1939. It was the first 'kill' by Günther Prien, who soon became a U-boat 'ace'. His success led Dönitz to recruit him for the dangerous mission to attack Scapa Flow.

The *Bosnia*, a Cunard White Star ship, was carrying a cargo of sulphur to Glasgow when it came under attack off the Portuguese coast. Prien first saw a 'plume of smoke', which he described as coming into view 'like a dragonfly flitting over a stream'. His submarine dived and he observed the ship through his periscope until it had passed clear of him. He then surfaced to the stern of the ship and fired a warning shot intended to show the captain of the *Bosnia* that he should surrender. When the ship ignored him Prien ordered a second round to be fired, but the captain still refused to surrender and tried to escape.

The *Bosnia* not only failed to stop but radioed for help while the U-boat fired warning shots. The third shot hit the vessel and started a fire, after which the crew lowered the lifeboats and prepared to abandon the ship, whose cargo of iron ore quickly made it unstable. Survivors took to the lifeboats and were rescued by a Norwegian vessel.

The *Bosnia* was on fire but it refused to sink, so Prien launched a torpedo. After it exploded the ship broke in half and within seconds it sank beneath the waves. Miraculously, only one member of the *Bosnia*'s crew died. Prien sank three ships before he was recalled to Kiel by Dönitz.[4]

His second victim tried to turn the tables on its attacker. When the *Gartavon* was waylaid by Prien the crew abandoned ship and took to the lifeboats, but not before its engines had been set to full steam ahead and its course altered so that it made directly for the U-boat. Prien took rapid evasive action and narrowly avoided being hit by the merchant ship. Furious at this near miss, he demanded that the captain identify himself. When he did so, he informed him that because he had committed a hostile act against him he would not radio for help but would instead tell the next neutral ship he encountered of the crew's plight. The captain then asked if he was free to row away and Prien gave his permission.[5]

THE DRIFT TOWARDS UNRESTRICTED SUBMARINE WARFARE

By 23 September 1939 a high-level discussion took place over the rules of engagement for U-boats. Dönitz complained to Raeder that British ships under attack always radioed for help, rather than surrendering and allowing the Germans to search and sink them. As a result, aircraft often attempted to attack U-boats while they were trying to stop the ships. As Dönitz pointed out to his superior officer, these actions were against international maritime law and endangered U-boat crews. Raeder agreed and spoke with Hitler, who authorized them to 'fire upon vessels which used their wireless'. Hitler refused to sanction unrestricted submarine warfare which was Dönitz's goal but the U-boat chief issued his own instructions to his crews.[6]

Dönitz decided to stretch Hitler's words to violate the spirit of international maritime law while sticking to its letter. He issued instructions to his U-boat crews authorizing them to sink merchant ships sailing without lights 'in sea areas where only English vessels are to be expected'. He added: 'Permission to take this step needs merely to be based on the unspoken approval of the naval operation staff. The sinking of a merchant ship must be justified in the War Plan as due to possible confusion with a warship or auxiliary cruiser.'[7]

The next day saw a further move towards unrestricted submarine warfare when a public statement declared that '… in waters around the British Isles and in the vicinity of the French coast, the safety of neutral ships can no longer be taken for granted'. This was a clear warning that neutral ships trading with Britain or France were regarded as legitimate targets for attack.[8]

Dönitz clarified the implications of this policy by ordering his crews to: 'rescue no one and take no one with you. Care only for your own boat and strive to achieve the next success as soon as possible.'[9]

October saw a further drift towards unrestricted U-boat warfare when instructions were given to ignore the Prize Regulations in the North Sea and the Baltic. Submarines were now allowed to attack any merchant ships in those areas without warning if they were armed or sailing without lights at night. Later that month this relaxation of the rules was extended to cover any ship belonging to an enemy nation. Hitler eventually lifted the ban on attacking passenger ships if they were British or French vessels.[10]

On 24 November an official statement by the German government warned that neutral ships operating in British or French waters could no longer assume they were safe from attack. By the end of November unrestricted submarine warfare had begun in all but name within those areas. The result was a dramatic increase in the number of ships sunk and lives lost. However, the British failed to adapt to the new situation and protection for merchantmen remained inadequate.[11]

SUBMARINE SHORTAGES

The shortage of suitable British escort ships was matched by the small number of submarines at Germany's disposal. Dönitz pleaded with Raeder to build a large fleet of U-boats, suggesting 300 vessels. He declared that with this vast flotilla he could strangle British trade and force the UK to surrender.

Raeder put Dönitz's ideas before Hitler but he was only a half-hearted advocate of submarines. Hitler was faced with demands from all of the services for equipment and training and the navy came a poor third in his thinking. Aircraft, tanks and heavy artillery were what he considered the decisive weapons for winning the war. He had no understanding of naval warfare and preferred Raeder's armada of surface ships to the cheaper and easily constructed submarines favoured by Dönitz. Hitler was most impressed by the aerial power of the Luftwaffe and so Dönitz's views, realistic though they were, found no support at the highest level.[12]

Not only were U-boats few in number but they also faced technical problems, with even surfaced submarines limited in speed and possessing a small stock of torpedoes. And in the early stages of the war torpedoes often malfunctioned, adding to the problems. The Germans also had little air cover while the RAF could offer protection to merchant ships.[13]

U-boats and their naval adversaries faced difficulties in detecting each other's presence. Naval intelligence on both sides, particularly the British, was patchy and ASDIC quickly proved fallible. Radar was some time away, although both sides had a precursor of the system. So with the vast expanse of ocean to patrol, both prey and predator frequently failed to find one another.[14]

Another problem for the British in terms of deploying convoys effectively was the shortage of trained signalmen. Crash training

View from on board a British ship as a convoy – comprising 24 merchantmen, mostly colliers – steams in line across the North Sea, 26 March 1940.

programmes were implemented but it soon became apparent that the inexperienced signalmen found it hard to observe and transmit adequately during darkness and bad weather. Fog, of course, made their task almost impossible.[15]

The result of these problems was two years of stalemate. Britain was unable to protect its merchant ships adequately but Germany could not sink enough vessels to force the British to surrender. There was an approximate 'balance of terror' between 1939 and 1941, with heavy casualties on both sides but neither combatant able to achieve victory.

In 1941 Britain was finally able to provide sufficient vessels to guard the merchant ships. Once the convoy system was properly implemented the balance of power in the war at sea began to shift in favour of the British rather than the Germans.

THE POLITICAL AND MILITARY BACKGROUND

In spite of his subsequent popularity Churchill made numerous enemies during his political career and the majority of Conservative MPs distrusted him as a maverick. When Chamberlain recalled him to the Admiralty there was considerable opposition in Tory ranks over his appointment.

Churchill had a good relationship with Sir Dudley Pound, who became First Sea Lord in June 1939. Pound's relationship with his subordinates is more contested. He was accused of 'back seat driving' by senior naval officers and clashed with the commanders of the Home Fleet. Nevertheless, Churchill saw him as a safe pair of hands and he worked so closely with him on naval strategy that he was nicknamed 'Churchill's anchor'.[16]

There are suggestions that Pound was able to temper Churchill's often impulsive decisions, but both men made errors of judgement in conducting the naval war. Churchill proposed a reckless plan known as Operation Catherine, which involved

Winston Churchill with Sir Dudley Pound on New Year's Day, 1940.

sending three heavily armed battleships into the Baltic Sea. They would have been supported by an aircraft carrier and other vessels in an attempt to prevent shipments of iron ore to Germany. The main source for the Nazis was neutral Sweden, so the plan was foolhardy and a violation of Swedish neutrality. Chamberlain and Pound combined to persuade Churchill that the scheme should be dropped but he remained determined to strike a blow against Germany by sea, particularly given the hiatus in land activity.[17]

As usual, Chamberlain hesitated about taking the offensive and blew hot and cold on all possible courses of action. One moment he discussed declaring war on the Soviet Union and the next ruled out laying mines. His reluctance to put the British economy on a war footing also constrained military activity; between September 1939 and March 1940 there was hardly any increase in government expenditure. Chamberlain was convinced that Germany could be defeated with little fighting if a naval blockade was maintained to strangle its imports.

Troopships carried British soldiers over to France but the men remained inactive, waiting for the order to attack. Within the British government there was a sense of paralysis. Declaring war on Germany and ferrying troops across the Channel seemed to be the limit of their ambitions.[18]

There were tensions in both the British and French governments over the best way to prosecute the war. Some of the attitudes of individual ministers seem incredible today. The RAF wasted precious fuel and pilots dropping propaganda leaflets over Germany and when the MP Leo Amery approached Sir Kingsley Wood, Minister for Air, suggesting that instead of dropping leaflets the planes should be bombing German factories his remarks were received with incredulity. Wood responded: 'But that's private property. You'll be asking me to bomb the Ruhr next!'[19]

While the government refused either to bomb Germany or send troops to invade it, the naval blockade showed some grasp of military reality. Otherwise, the level of forward planning by both Britain and France was almost non-existent, with one unrealistic scheme after another being proposed and rejected.

PLANNED TAKEOVER OF SCANDINAVIA

Scandinavia was the focus of most of these phantom operations. Following the Soviet invasion of Finland in 1939, variations on plans to conquer it were considered by Chamberlain and his Cabinet. They were willing to violate international law by invading neutral countries, which showed the hollowness of their pretence of the moral high ground over Poland. By declaring war on Germany and promising to assist Poland they led the Poles to resist longer than necessary in the false hope of help from the West, which never came. Having failed to help the Poles against the Nazis, the Russian invasion of Finland made them consider several unfeasible options. It was proposed that Scapa Flow would be the main base to launch an attack on Norway, Denmark, Sweden, the Faroe Islands and Iceland so they could then drive the Russians out of Finland. The theory was that by liberating Finland and occupying the rest of Scandinavia, German imports by sea could be virtually stopped and Hitler might be forced to sue for peace.[20]

The fact that these actions were as contrary to international law as the invasions of Poland and Finland was a marginal concern for the governments. And the risk of war with the Soviet Union was overlooked or treated lightly.[21]

Russian troops performed poorly against the Finns and the war dragged on for almost four months. Chamberlain continued to hesitate over the planned invasion and he did not finally agree to the plans until late March. Churchill believed the operation was unviable but events overtook the planners as Germany invaded Denmark and Norway themselves. With the British and Germans having considered conquering the country, it is not surprising that when the invasion came and the king of Norway was woken from sleep and told his country was at war, he replied: 'Who with?'

Although Churchill had opposed the planned takeover of Scandinavia, a risky and illegal plan of his own was rejected by Chamberlain. In the first month of the war he suggested setting mines in the Norwegian Leads around Narvik. The plan was dangerous and contrary to international law, but it might have worked in the short term. In the longer term, though, by violating Norwegian neutrality it was illegal and risked retaliation against Britain. Sweden might have cut off supplies to the British altogether and Britain's attempts to charter Norwegian merchant ships to strengthen its own merchant navy would have been futile if the waters had been mined. As it was, when the Norwegian and Swedish governments were approached they refused to allow the mines to be placed.[22]

The rejection of Churchill's scheme led to an even more bizarre plan. This time it was put forward by French strategists, who favoured invading Norway and Finland and taking control of the Swedish mines. They proposed sending French naval vessels to the north of Finland.[23]

These and similar variations on unworkable schemes were formulated, considered, reconsidered and refined. It was not until 18 February 1940, three months after the Russian invasion of Finland and six months after the rejection of Churchill's plan to mine Norwegian waters, that an invasion plan was agreed in principle. On 15 March the ships were waiting in Scotland and the troops were ready to embark. Then, after four months of fighting, the Finns surrendered to the Russians. Probably with some relief, the invasion was called off. It would have led to an embarrassing defeat and ran the risk of war with the Soviet Union.

Yet again muddle, confusion and dithering held back any idea of offensive action against Germany. There were severe difficulties with any of the possible courses of action but inaction and failure to strike at the enemy made things worse than necessary. The failure to act was in many respects even more disastrous than the bungled operations that never saw the light of day.[24]

THE NAVAL BLOCKADE OF GERMANY

From late 1937 Sir Frederick Leith-Ross, the principal economic adviser to the British government, became convinced that war with Germany was inevitable. He then approached the government with a plan to institute an economic blockade of Germany enforced by the Royal Navy, believing that it would be an effective method of curtailing German strength. His idea was that by using new technology and treating the large British overseas businesses as intelligence-gathering centres, in places like New York, Buenos Aires, Rio de Janeiro and even Tokyo and Rome, the Navy could act upon advanced knowledge of any ships carrying war materials to Germany before they set sail.

When Leith-Ross put his proposal to Chamberlain in 1937, it was rejected out of hand. Chamberlain preferred to continue with his policy of appeasement and only after its failure did he finally recognize the need to prepare for war. In April 1939 a joint staff paper was issued by French and British military leaders suggesting that economic war might be an effective weapon against German aggression. The known dependence of the Germans on imports of raw materials would hurt them more severely than the Western Allies.[25]

On the outbreak of war on 3 September 1939, Britain and (until its surrender in the summer of 1940) France instituted an economic blockade of Germany. They adopted a variety of methods to prevent the Nazis from receiving food, metals, minerals and other essential supplies. One of them was to buy as many necessities as possible from neutral countries to prevent the Germans from obtaining them. Britain in particular paid inflated prices in an attempt to corner the market. A direct blockade involved intercepting neutral merchant ships and seizing their cargo if it was intended for Germany.[26]

The consequences of this curtailment of supplies contributed to the German invasion of Norway and Denmark in 1940. Scandinavia was a crucial supply route for the Germans and the British and French attempted to choke off deliveries to them. They reduced supplies to an extent, but until June 1941 Germany could import substantial amounts of crucial raw materials from the Soviet Union. Spanish harbours were then used to transport weapons and essential supplies to Germany.

On 4 September the Admiralty formally announced that all merchant vessels would be examined by the Contraband Control Service of the Navy and the French Blockade Ministry, whose own ships were, by joint agreement, placed under British control. A list of items regarded as contraband and therefore liable to confiscation included food, animal fodder and clothing and the materials used in the production of these substances. More obvious contraband items were ammunition, explosives, chemicals, fuel, communications equipment, means of transport, money and bullion.[27]

The Navy assigned three places as centres for Contraband Control. Weymouth and The Downs were designated to cover the English Channel and Kirkwall in the Orkney Islands was given the role of monitoring the North Sea. Ships sailing directly to Allied ports were not unduly inconvenienced but those on other routes were stopped at the Contraband Control centre, where they were subjected to detailed scrutiny.[28]

Three more contraband centres to inspect ships were set up in the Mediterranean. Gibraltar controlled access into and out of the western Mediterranean and Haifa the eastern section, while Aden controlled access to the Suez Canal. Britain and France worked jointly to patrol the Mediterranean and Red Sea areas and Britain's control of the Suez Canal meant that its supply lines were secure.[29]

The introduction of these measures infuriated neutral nations. Scandinavian countries and the Dutch regularly traded with Germany and were irate at having their ships stopped and searched by customs officers and their cargo confiscated. Even without this the delays led to perishable cargo rotting and no compensation was paid by the British or French governments to the neutrals affected by the ban.

At first ships tried to avoid these inspections but the excellent intelligence network set up by Leith-Ross meant the British had prior knowledge of their destination and often the contents of the ship. After initial protests, neutral captains learned it was better and quicker to co-operate with the Contraband Control. Supported by the Navy, they forced neutral ships into one of the designated ports for their inspection and this reduced German imports considerably.

Ships stopping at one of the Control ports had to raise a red and white flag with a blue border. This was a signal that it was ready to be examined. When it was dark those in the port used lights to warn an approaching vessel that it must stop. The ship's 'control' flag had to remain raised until the ship had been cleared. In the Boarding Room of the port the arrangements for the boarding and examination of ships were made. Ships were evaluated by a team

British sailors board a Dutch ship as part of Contraband Control operations, 1940.

of eight men, who inspected the manifest, documents and other necessary papers. The radio cabin was sealed to prevent signals being sent while the ship was undergoing inspection. If all was well, the boarding party returned to shore and sent the Ministry of Economic Warfare the details of the passengers, manifest, port of origin and destination via teleprinter. Once the Ministry gave its permission the papers were returned to the ship's captain and he received a clearance certificate. If things were found 'not in order' then the cargo and even the ship could be confiscated.[30]

During the first four weeks of war the British confiscated nearly 300,000 tons (272,000 tonnes) of contraband and the French 100,000 tons (91,000 tonnes). The Ministry issued quotas to nations known to be trading with Germany and warned them that exceeding the permitted quantities would incur severe penalties. In the first 15 weeks of the war the British and French confiscated 870,000 tons (789,000 tonnes) of goods, representing 10 per cent of German imports and clients who had been servicing Germany for years began to cease doing so, for fear of having their cargo seized. All of this meant that the blockade was severely affecting the German capability to wage war.[31]

GERMAN COUNTERMEASURES TO THE BLOCKADE

Even before the war Germany tried to make itself as self-sufficient as possible. Imports had been steadily reduced and the massive production of synthetic substitutes for various items was undertaken. Trading deals were made with Romania (the main supplier of oil to Germany), Sweden, Spain, Finland, Turkey and Yugoslavia, in order to allow Germany to stockpile scarce items such as nickel, cotton, wool and tungsten and plans were put in place to grow sunflowers and soya beans in Romania.

In spite of these measures, rationing was strictly enforced even before the war and there were shortages of certain items.

Park railings were removed to be melted down for possible military use and it was recognized that it might be necessary to occupy Yugoslavia, Romania and Hungary so their resources could be controlled in the event of an Allied blockade.

Once the war began the Nazis immediately denounced the blockade as illegal, but they worked hard to circumvent it. They then attempted to set up a blockade of their own by insisting that all neutral traffic coming via the Baltic Sea had to pass through the Kiel Canal for inspection. This primarily affected the Scandinavian countries, who were big suppliers of wood pulp to Britain, which was used partly for newsprint and partly for explosives.

The Germans began to sink ships carrying wood pulp from Norway, Sweden and Finland to Britain. This continued until Sweden threatened to cut off supplies of iron ore to Germany unless the attacks on its ships ceased. Germany then began seizing Danish ships carrying foodstuffs to Britain and by 21 September 1939 over 300 British ships and over 1,000 neutral ships had been detained by the Germans, 66 of which had their cargo confiscated.[32]

The Nazi–Soviet pact brought considerable economic advantages to Germany. Romania, effectively a satellite state of Germany, had been supplying it with oil for years, but now the vast natural resources of the Soviet Union were also available, which helped make up for the shortage of Germany's own resources. Russia supplied the Germans with oil and grain and provided facilities for German U-boats and ships to be refuelled and repaired at its Arctic port of Teriberka to the east of Murmansk. In addition, the Americans sold wheat, petrol, rubber and tin to the Russians, which they sold on to Germany. The influx of raw materials assisted the Germans in countering the effects of the blockade.[33]

Initially the blockade appeared to be successful and large quantities of contraband were seized. For all the British efforts the initial optimism that purely economic measures could bring Germany to the peace table evaporated by early 1940. It was clear that Germany was continuing to import and neutral countries were openly flouting the British ban on trade with the Germans. Sweden refused to agree to a British request to stop supplying iron ore to the Nazis, but other countries used neutral countries to evade the blockade. Holland was dependent on German trade and supplied oil, diamonds, copper and tin via America. Norway, Sweden and Switzerland then increased their purchases of these items as well as buying steel, copper, petrol and cotton – all prohibited items – and the British were aware that their destination was Germany.

In spite of the prohibition on supplying arms to combatants through the Neutrality Act imposed on the United States, there was no such ban on raw materials. American firms sold large quantities of these to neutral countries, knowing they would be resold to Germany. In addition, the Balkan states of Romania, Bulgaria and Yugoslavia exported oil, bauxite, maize, wheat, meat, tobacco, chromium and other items, and Greece and Turkey supplied the Germans with a variety of necessities. Collectively these purchases enabled Germany to withstand the blockade.[34]

Recognizing the problem, Britain tried to use its financial muscle to prevent the Germans from obtaining the goods they needed. This took the form of overpaying and underselling in these markets, in an attempt to discourage traders from selling to Germany. This was successful in some areas but the Romanians were so frightened of the German and Russian troops nearby that they eventually threw themselves completely on to the German side and refused to sell oil to Britain. This impacted considerably on Britain's resources but its oil shortages were never as severe as those of the Germans. Without Russian and Romanian oil, they were in no position to continue an extended war.

THE AMERICAN REACTION TO THE BLOCKADE

Passenger ships as well as merchant ships had to submit to Contraband Control. Luggage and particularly mail and parcels interested them and any of these items that were addressed to Germany were opened by the customs inspectors, to the intense anger of the Americans. By late November 1939 over 60 American ships had been stopped and searched and the owners demanded that the US government should exert diplomatic pressure on the British. As a result, on 22 December 1939 the State Department made a formal protest, which was ignored by the British government.[35]

Then on 30 December the *Manhattan* sailed from New York destined for Italy. It was stopped six days into its voyage at Gibraltar and in spite of protests by the captain to the American Consul it was held up for 40 hours while it was searched. Over 200 bags of mail addressed to Germany were removed.[36]

This led to calls by aggrieved ship owners for the mail to be carried on US warships in future. Even when American ships were on the homeward leg of a journey to Germany their vessel was searched a second time. On 22 January the State Department repeated its protest, handing the UK ambassador to America a formal note demanding that the practice should be stopped. This caused panic in the British government and provoked a direct conflict between the Foreign Office and the Ministry of Economic Warfare. While the Foreign Office was terrified of turning the US against Britain, the Economic Warfare Ministry felt the benefits of the search and seizure policy outweighed the diplomatic risks. However, the British government as a whole sided with the continuation of the policy and declared that they had – presumably through intelligence sources – uncovered a widespread conspiracy by elements in the US to send contraband goods like soap, coffee, chocolate, food, clothing, jewellery, cash and bonds to Germany through the mail. Whether or not this was true – and the evidence suggests that it *was* – made little difference, as the British refused to back down and the policy continued, with American protests ignored and US vessels still subject to search and seizure. When an American flying boat was stopped and searched and its mail confiscated, the US government banned the sending of parcels overseas through air mail.[37]

In spite of this friction between the two nations Roosevelt persuaded Congress to pass an amendment to the Neutrality Act allowing combatants to purchase weapons provided they paid for them on a 'Cash and Carry' basis. This required them to pay in cash and collect the material themselves, an arrangement which in theory applied to all belligerents but in reality favoured Britain. The British had the financial resources and the ships to carry the arms across the ocean whereas the Germans had little foreign exchange or gold reserves and it was impossible for their ships to transport goods across the Atlantic. Even though British ships had to run the gauntlet of U-boats, mines and, to a lesser extent, surface warships, the majority of the purchased armaments were safely collected and brought back to the United Kingdom.[38]

THE NAVAL WAR INTENSIFIES

On 14 September *U-39* attacked the *Ark Royal* but its torpedoes missed the target. Depth charges fired by the destroyers escorting the aircraft carrier forced the submarine to the surface and the crew were taken prisoner, making *U-39* the first German naval casualty of the war.[39]

The first Allied convoy, HX-1, sailed from Halifax in Canada on 16 September. It was made up of 14 British and three French vessels. All of the vessels made it safely to Liverpool on 30 September, though one of the French ships in the convoy, the *Vermont*, was torpedoed the following month. By the end of September 50 British and French ships were sunk, with a loss of over 200,000 tons, but only two U-boats were lost.

October was a difficult month with 34 Allied ships totalling 185,000 tons sunk while the Germans lost five U-boats. In November Britain and France lost 29 ships totalling almost 78,000 tons while the Germans lost a single U-boat.[40] The end of the month saw Britain and France lose 43 ships with a tonnage of 108,347 tons and Germany again only lost a single U-boat. During the whole of 1939, the Allies only achieved limited success in the naval war, as most offensive actions by the British and French ended in failure. On the other hand, the German navy was encouraged by the decline in supplies reaching Britain. In spite of Germany's successes there was no progress towards peace, which remained Hitler's priority, and Germany had only inflicted pinpricks on the Allies, rather than striking mortal blows.

ALLIED LOSSES IN 1940

The beginning of 1940 saw the British and French losing 56 ships in January with a tonnage of 173,996 tons, while the Germans lost only two U-boats. In February 1940 came Hitler's directive authorizing unrestricted submarine warfare. The same month saw the *Altmark* incident (described in the following chapter), which precipitated the German decision to invade Norway. And on 11 March a Blenheim bomber sank *U-31* in the Jade Bight area, killing the crew of 58.[41]

The imbalance of casualties and losses continued throughout March with the British and French having 26 ships with a tonnage of 73,071 tons sunk while the Germans lost three U-boats.[42] Naval activity in April was centred around Norway, where the British inflicted heavy losses on the Germans. In spite of their success, other developments forced them to retreat and the Norwegian campaign was a failure. German naval success continued, with May seeing the Allies losing 16 ships with a tonnage of 63,476 tons and the Germans a single U-boat. During the course of June the British and French lost 62 ships with a total tonnage of 335,319 tons. The Germans lost a single U-boat.[43]

July saw intense naval activity, with the passenger liner *Arandora Star* being sunk off the coast of Ireland by a U-boat. It was carrying 1,500 German and Italian prisoners from the UK to camps in Canada. Although 857 survivors were rescued by a Canadian destroyer, the remainder of the people on the ship died.[44]

By the end of the month the Allies had lost 41 ships with a total tonnage of 203,709 tons and the Germans two U-boats.[45] In the same month, Hitler gave the order for Operation Sea Lion to begin, though at this stage it was still in the planning phase. August saw further Allied losses, with 57 ships sunk for the loss of two U-boats. The pattern was repeated in September with 57 ships sunk and one U-boat lost. However, the failure of the Luftwaffe to defeat the RAF and make it safe for naval forces to transport troops across the English Channel forced Hitler to postpone Operation Sea Lion. In spite of the abandonment of the project, the Admiralty remained reluctant to provide sufficient protection for convoys and instead focused its attention on the perceived need to defend home waters against possible invasion.[46]

The losses continued in September, with 57 ships totalling 385,152 tons sunk for the loss of one U-boat. Things did not improve in October, which saw the destruction of most of convoy SC-7 and a further 72 ships sunk for the loss of a single U-boat.[47] Then in November the cargo ship *Casanare* and the armed merchant cruisers *Laurentic* and HMS *Patroclus* were sunk by a U-boat, in spite of destroyers and aircraft attacking the submarine during the combat.[48]

The Italians fared much worse than the Germans in the naval war. On 6 November the Italian submarine *Faa di Bruno* was sunk off the coast of Ireland by the Canadian destroyer *Ottawa* and the British destroyer *Harvester*.[49] Another disaster for the Italians occurred when the aircraft carrier *Illustrious* launched 21 Fairey Swordfish aircraft against the Italian fleet at Taranto. Four ships were damaged or sunk but two aircraft were shot down by anti-aircraft defences.[50]

A serious intelligence failure resulted on 11 November when the German ship *Atlantis* captured the British merchant ship *Automedon* on its way to Singapore while carrying classified documents, revealing the poor state of Allied defences in the Far East. The Germans passed the information they gained on to the Japanese and it made their attacks on British possessions in 1941 much easier.[51]

By the end of the month the Allies lost 33 ships and the Germans two U-boats. The loss of ships continued in December with mixed fortunes for both sides.

The Italian submarine *Argo* torpedoed the Canadian destroyer *Saguenay* and killed 21 crew members but failed to sink the ship and by the end of December 41 Allied ships had been sunk with no German losses. One Italian submarine was destroyed.[52]

The year closed on a bleak note for Britain with U-boats and German naval vessels inflicting an unsustainable rate of casualties. Without the 50 destroyers sent by the United States the British could not have survived more than a few months.

NOTES

1 Max Caulfield, *A Night of Terror: The Story of the Athenia affair*, Muller, 1958
2 Anonymous account by a survivor of the sinking of the *Athenia*, Imperial War Museum
3 Robert Glenton, *The Royal Oak Affair: The Saga of Admiral Collard and Bandmaster Barnacle*, Leo Cooper, 1991
4 Günther Prien, *Fortunes of War – U-boat Commander*, Tempus, 2000
5 Ibid.
6 Padfield, *Dönitz*
7 Ibid.
8 Ibid.
9 Ibid.
10 Ibid.
11 Ibid.
12 Ibid.
13 Ibid.
14 Ibid.
15 Padfield, *War Beneath the Sea*
16 Robin Brodhurst, *Churchill's Anchor: A Biography of Admiral of the Fleet Sir Dudley Pound*, Pen and Sword, 2000
17 Markku Ruotsila, *Churchill and Finland: A Study in Anticommunism and Geopolitics*, Routledge, 2005
18 Edward Spears, *Assignment to Catastrophe, Volume I: Prelude to Dunkirk July 1939–May 1940*, Heinemann, 1954
19 Max Jacobson, *The Diplomacy of the Winter War: The Soviet Attack on Finland 1939–1940*, Harvard University Press, 1961
20 Vaino Tanner, *The Winter War: Finland against Russia 1939–1940*, Stanford University Press, 1957
21 S.W. Roskill, *War at Sea 1939–1945, Volume 1, The Defensive*, HMSO, 1954
22 Ibid.
23 Ibid.
24 Ibid.
25 J.R.M. Butler, *History of the Second World War, Grand Strategy, Volume II*, HMSO, 1976
26 Thomas Munch-Petersen, *The Strategy of Phoney War: Britain, Sweden and the Iron Ore Question 1939–1940*, Militärhistoriska studier, 1981
27 Vincent J. Esposito (ed.), *A Concise History of World War II*, Praeger Publishers, 1964
28 Robert K. Massie, *Castles of Steel: Britain, Germany and the Winning of the Great War at Sea*, Ballantine Books, 2004
29 'Fleet Begins the Blockade', *Daily Express*, 4 September 1939

30 Frederick Sondern, 'Contraband Control: England's Ministry of Economic Warfare Seeks a Death Grip on Germany's Trade', *Life*, vol. 8, no. 3, 15 January 1940

31 'Getting a Stranglehold on German Commerce', *The War Illustrated*, vol. 1, no. 7, 28 October 1939

32 *Time*, 8 January 1940, vol. XXXV, no. 2

33 Edward E. Ericson, *Feeding the German Eagle: Soviet Economic Aid to Nazi Germany, 1933–1941*, Greenwood Publishing Group, 1999

34 *Time*, 25 September 1939, vol. XXXIV, no. 13

35 *Time*, 9 October 1939, vol. XXXIV, no. 15

36 'Americans Get Hot Under the Collar as British Keep Seizing U.S. Mail', *Life*, vol. 8, no. 6, 5 February 1940

37 *Time*, 5 February 1940, vol. XXXV, no. 6

38 Robert Divine, *Roosevelt and World War II*, Johns Hopkins University Press, 1969

39 Gröner, *German Warships: 1815–1945*, Naval Inst. Press, 1990

40 Bruce Watson, *Atlantic Convoys and Nazi Raiders*, Praeger, 2006

41 Paul Kemp, *U-Boats Destroyed – German Submarine Losses in the World Wars*, Arms and Armour, 1999

42 Padfield, *War Beneath the Sea*

43 Ibid.

44 Ibid.

45 Ibid.

46 Ibid.

47 Ibid.

48 Jack Greene and Alessandro Massignani, *The Naval War in the Mediterranean, 1940–1943*, Chatham Publishing, 1998

49 http://www.sommergibili.com/faadibrunoe.htm/

50 Thomas P. Lowry and John W.G. Wellham, *The Attack on Taranto: Blueprint for Pearl Harbor*, Stackpole Books, 1995

51 Padfield, *War Beneath the Sea*

52 Ibid.

CHAPTER THREE

ORGANIZING THE NAVAL WAR

Britain and France declared war on Germany in September 1939 but only at sea was there any fighting. Chamberlain clung to the hope that Hitler could be defeated without substantial military activity and his Cabinet contained supporters of the policy of appeasement.

Churchill, though back in the Cabinet, remained disliked and distrusted by most ministers and many MPs and his bellicose and prickly personality made him a difficult colleague. He pressed for active measures to be taken against Germany and refused to consider the possibility of defeat. But even with its empire to support it the British nation was in desperate danger and its isolation – worse after the collapse of France – made it vulnerable. The French blew hot and cold on military action and their navy barely saw combat before the fall of France while Britain's army was small and its navy was overstretched. The fleet was largely required to defend home waters and there were few planes available to provide air cover for ships.

THE BRITISH SUBMARINE FLOTILLA
The British submarine force was small and ineffective. When war broke out only 18 submarines were available for the European and Atlantic theatres, as the bulk of Britain's

submarine flotilla was based in Singapore in anticipation of a Japanese attack. The small number of boats available was compounded by poor training and a lack of awareness in the Admiralty of their proper role.[1]

Some British submarines were sent to patrol the coasts of Norway and Holland. They were enlisted to enforce the naval blockade and act as spies, reporting any sightings of German warships. The boats patrolling Norway were placed so closely together that when poor visibility and a communications breakdown occurred on 10 September the result was tragedy. In the war's first instance of 'friendly fire', the submarine *Triton* sank its sister boat *Oxley*. Only two members of the crew survived.[2]

Another danger to British submarines, particularly in poor weather, was the high risk of being mistakenly attacked by RAF bombers. Coastal Command, at that time responsible for air cover, possessed ageing aircraft whose primary role was reconnaissance rather than combat. None of its air crews were trained in attacking U-boats or the protection of ships. Their bombs were aimed purely by 'sight' and were nearly always inaccurate, with a single submarine sunk by Coastal Command bombers in the first eight months of the war. It was not until summer 1940 that depth charges for aircraft were introduced and they were not generally adopted until spring 1941. A great opportunity had been lost to modernize and streamline British submarines and the aerial side of anti-submarine warfare. Once again, the antiquated thinking of the Navy was the principal reason for this failure.[3]

THE PHONEY WAR

In the period from September 1939 to May 1940, known as the Phoney War, France and Germany both seemed to be waiting for the other side to attack. Britain confined itself to naval activities and its troops remained idle in France while the RAF was hardly engaged in meaningful activity. Only at sea was there real conflict. Even the Germans, having invaded and conquered Poland, seemed reluctant to engage in serious military action. Hitler still believed that a peace treaty was possible while the Allies remained content to fight a purely defensive campaign.

On 19 February 1940, a fleet of German destroyers sailed into the North Sea on what was known as Operation Wikinger. It was intended to prevent British submarines and fishing boats from operating in the Dogger Bank region. The mission was a fiasco, with two of the destroyers sunk at sea through mines and bombing by the Luftwaffe, which mistook them for British ships. Almost 600 German sailors perished in this venture and the plan was abandoned. The only result of the attempt was that German pilots and mines had destroyed two of their own ships and killed many of their own troops.[4]

THE *ALTMARK* INCIDENT

Towards the end of 1939 the German ship *Altmark* took aboard 299 British prisoners. They were survivors from ships sunk by the *Graf Spee* and were being transported back to Germany. When the vessel reached the neutral waters of Norway the Norwegians, at the request of the British, investigated it three times and declared that there was neither contraband nor prisoners of war on board. Whether this was simply the result of negligence or outright collaboration with the Germans is unclear but certainly the hold – containing the British prisoners – was never searched and the Norwegian inspectors appeared willing to accept German assurances about the contents of the ship. The prisoners tried to signal their presence to the Norwegian inspectors but their attempts were either not heard or ignored, depending on whether incompetence or collusion was to blame.

The Royal Navy refused to accept the Norwegians' assurances and sent ships to pursue the *Altmark*. RAF reconnaissance planes finally discovered the vessel and the Navy set out to locate it. They found it moored in the Jøssingfjord and managed to trap it. Unable to escape, the ship's captain was issued with a demand by the British to allow them to inspect it. This was refused and Norwegian naval vessels blocked British attempts to enter and search the *Altmark*. When they aimed their torpedoes at the *Cossack*, a British destroyer, the captain asked for instructions from the Admiralty. They responded with the following order:

> *Unless Norwegian torpedo-boat undertakes to convoy* Altmark *to Bergen with a joint Anglo-Norwegian guard on board, and a joint escort, you should board* Altmark, *liberate the prisoners, and take possession of the ship pending further instructions. If Norwegian torpedo-boat interferes, you should warn her to stand off. If she fires upon you, you should not reply unless attack is serious, in which case you should defend yourself, using no more force than is necessary, and ceasing fire when she desists. Suggest to Norwegian destroyer that honour is served by submitting to superior force.*

The Norwegians, unwilling to risk taking on a British destroyer, gave in. *Cossack* then sent a boarding party to the *Altmark* who encountered fierce resistance, which forced them to engage in hand to hand fighting. During the struggle eight German sailors were killed and ten wounded and a British sailor and a Norwegian sailor were also wounded.

From the legal point of view both Britain and Germany had violated international maritime law. It was illegal for the Germans to transport the British captives across the ocean to Norway and then lie about the contents of their ship. On the other hand, the British action was a clear violation of Norwegian neutrality.

Once the crew of the *Altmark* had been overcome the British boarding party shouted: 'Any Englishmen here?' The loud cry from the prisoners, 'Yes! We are all British!' led to cheers from their rescuers.

Protests from Germany and Norway followed but the Norwegians were anxious to avoid becoming involved in the war and confined themselves to verbal objections to the British action. It created disquiet about neutrality and the treatment neutrals could expect, not only from pro-German countries.

On the home front it was one of the few 'actions' during the Phoney War and it had an uplifting effect on morale. The British media engaged in massive exaggeration, with fictitious stories of atrocities against the prisoners and inhuman conditions on board the German ship. A popular song was written comparing the actions of the *Cossack* with the naval triumphs of Drake and Nelson.

The longer-term consequences were to encourage both Germany and Britain to consider occupying Norway in order to control the flow of Swedish iron ore. It is doubtful whether the British plans would have worked but events were soon out of their hands as the Germans, fearing the loss of that vital raw material, launched a pre-emptive invasion of their own. In a lightning campaign which caught Britain and France by surprise they occupied Norway and Denmark with token resistance. Now the British were forced to consider a counter-attack, but as with most of their plans in the early stages of the war, this turned out to be a disastrous mistake.[5]

THE NARVIK FIASCO

The British response to the German conquest of Norway and Denmark was to launch an invasion of Norway themselves. It began by adopting the rejected proposal of Churchill to mine Norwegian waters but also involved committing significant amounts of British troops and naval strength to the enterprise. The idea was to use the city of Narvik as a base for an attempt to recapture Norway from the Germans.[6]

On 10 October 1939 Raeder suggested to Hitler that Germany should capture the ports along the coast of Norway. He maintained that this action, which he admitted 'breaks all rules of naval warfare', would safeguard the imports of iron ore from Sweden and provide bases from which the navy could strike out into the Atlantic. Raeder told Hitler that seizing Norwegian ports would have a 'decisive' effect on the naval war.[7]

Göring and Keitel disagreed and focused their energies on a land war supported by the Luftwaffe. In spite of the fact that Raeder repeated his demands for an invasion of Norway after the Russian attack on Finland Hitler rejected his idea, but as the news of British plans to invade leaked out he changed his mind.

On 1 March 1940, following the encounter between the *Cossack* and the *Altmark*, Raeder was authorized to issue an order for the invasion of Norway. But on 8 April British destroyers began laying mines in the waters leading to the port at Narvik. Unknown to them the majority of the German navy's ships were already en route to Norway. On the following day, 9 April, ten German destroyers arrived at Narvik and occupied the port with minimal resistance. The British had been outwitted and had to improvise countermeasures. Once again, both the planning and the execution of their schemes were poorly handled.[8]

In an ill-advised move, on 10 April three British destroyers entered Narvik. Their arrival took the Germans by surprise and they sank two ships before shore batteries opened fire and several German destroyers appeared. The result was the sinking of two British ships with 17 men killed and two missing, after which the surviving ships, badly damaged, made their escape.

Stunned by the disaster, Churchill ordered the destruction of every German vessel in Narvik. On 13 April a battleship, an aircraft carrier and nine destroyers entered the harbour and began their attack.[9]

As the ships entered they were bombarded by shore batteries and German warships. The battle was fierce and when it was over eight German destroyers had been sunk or crippled and one U-boat sunk at a cost of three British destroyers.[10] At this point there was a real chance of winning the Norwegian campaign but a breakdown in communications and an over-cautious attitude made this impossible. The naval forces were instructed 'to turn the enemy out of Narvik at the earliest possible moment' but by contrast the army told its forces that 'it is not intended that you should land in the face of opposition'.[11]

On 15 April the officer in charge of the soldiers, Major-General Mackesy, met with the naval commander, Admiral the Earl of Cork. They disagreed over their course of action. Cork demanded an immediate invasion while Mackesy declared it was too dangerous to launch an assault on the town. To the fury of Cork and Churchill, Mackesy refused to move until the snows cleared, but the weather grew worse and fresh snow fell. The Germans consolidated their control of Narvik while the admiral and the general argued.[12]

The deadlock between Cork and Mackesy led to the formulation of a new plan known as Operation Hammer. It was a reckless scheme to capture Trondheim, a port 500 miles

(800 km) south of Narvik. Churchill favoured the Narvik attack but was overruled. The plan was approved on 17 April but on the next day senior naval officers rejected it as too dangerous.[13] However, they put forward an alternative plan that was equally mistaken and reckless. The new suggestion was to split the attack on Trondheim into two forces, one to the north and the other to the south of the port. Two troopships en route to Narvik were made to change course and land on an island port. After they had been joined by British, French and Polish soldiers they advanced on Trondheim. However, the troops were harassed by the Luftwaffe and were unable to outfight the German soldiers. Ten days after the troops had landed the advance was stopped and by 2 May they had been forced to evacuate. Hundreds of soldiers had died needlessly and Trondheim remained under German control.[14]

At the end of May, Churchill, now prime minister, dismissed Mackesy and replaced him with General Auchinleck. As the Navy still controlled the port of Narvik, Auchinleck was able to lead his troops in a successful attack on the town. Narvik was at last in British hands, but it was a Pyrrhic victory in every way. At a cost of over 6,000 lives Narvik had been captured, but the blitzkrieg in the West meant the troops were urgently required in France and had to be evacuated. A successful British campaign in Norway might have brought Germany to its knees by cutting off its sea routes and stifling the supply of iron ore. Raeder was right to stress its vital importance for German survival and British indecision, confusion and a succession of poorly planned schemes resulted in a stunning triumph for Germany and a humiliating defeat for the British.[15]

The one bright spot for the British was that German U-boats had been largely ineffective during the Norwegian campaign as they had only sunk one ship. The problem was quickly identified as faulty torpedoes and it was soon corrected, but it is hard to imagine that the British would have come as close to success as they did if the U-boats had been able to operate at maximum effectiveness.[16]

Further comfort for the British was that the naval side of their operation had been a triumph. German losses were significant with ten destroyers, several support ships and one submarine sunk whereas they only sank two Allied ships and damaged several others. If the ground forces had been as effective as the Navy the Germans would have been driven out of Norway, but a combination of poor planning and indecision allowed them to recover and eventually the British and French forces were compelled to evacuate.[17]

The German attack on Holland, Belgium and France had achieved such momentum that it became more urgent for the British and the French to defend in the West than attempt to drive the Nazis out of Norway. Otherwise they might well have been successful in recapturing the country, in spite of poor planning and tactical mistakes.

General Walter Warlimont, deputy chief of the OKW, believed the German invasion of Norway was a mistake and that an immediate assault on Holland, Belgium and France would have made it unnecessary. The French would still have been defeated and Norway could have been occupied at leisure and at less cost. It was a hugely expensive venture for the Germans in terms of casualties and the loss of vital ships. On the other hand, a policy of inaction might have allowed the British and the French to cut off the vital iron ore supply, which would have hampered the invasion of France.

Both sides fought a poor campaign but the inability of U-boats alone to defeat the Royal Navy was clearly demonstrated. The main advantage the Germans gained from the Narvik fiasco was that they were able to use the country as a base for their ships and U-boats. Not only that, but the supply of iron ore from Sweden could no longer be threatened by the British.

For both sides the Norwegian campaign was a costly failure. Although the Germans held on to their bases in Norway until the end of the war, the cost in lives, maintenance and unnecessary expenditure did not justify the effort in conquering the country.

THE MERCHANT NAVY

The term 'merchant navy' was an invention of the press. It covered an assortment of vessels ranging from dilapidated tramp steamers to luxury liners, which were owned by a variety of companies ranging from exploitative small ship owners at one end of the spectrum to the White Star and P&O lines at the other.

The 1930s had plunged the shipping industry into a depression, so many vessels were laid up with insufficient cargoes to fill them. Crews were also left idle and when war came and the ships were suddenly in demand there was a shortage of hands. The result was that 15- and 16-year-old boys found themselves serving as deck hands and radio officers while men in their seventies already receiving their pensions were hauled out of retirement to serve once more.

Merchant seamen were aware that they were as much despised by the sailors of the Royal Navy as they were by their employers. However, the outbreak of war exposed them to dangers beyond the ordinary hazards of stormy weather. Worse still, the sailors in the merchant service had not been trained or prepared for the onslaught on them by U-boats and the Luftwaffe.

Captain Jack Broome, whose escort groups in the Arctic provided protection to the merchant ships, wrote some years later:

Smoke from a British merchant ship which was bombed because it was part of an Allied convoy on its way to the Soviet Union, 1942.

For years we had turned up our snobbish noses and maintained that the Merchant Navy was something to be seen and not heard. It was entirely our fault that they thought that we thought we were some superior form of sea life.[18]

Rear Admiral Sir Kenelm Creighton condemned the ship owners for their treatment of the crews, declaring that:

There were many disgracefully unseaworthy ships at sea flying the red ensign. Any merchant ship that managed to assemble with a convoy was automatically covered by government insurance. Certain unscrupulous British shipowners whose consciences did not boggle at the idea of gambling with the lives of seamen, were despicable enough to send ships not up to the standard needed to battle against the fury of the gales that haunt the Western Ocean in winter, ships that were not fit to be anywhere but in a breaker's yard.[19]

Even women sailed as merchant seamen, mainly on ocean liners and passenger ships. Their role was normally as stewardesses, laundresses and nurses but a tiny handful worked in more responsible positions. Twenty-two Canadian women served, mainly on Norwegian vessels, as radio operators. All but one survived the war and the only exception was Maude Stean, who was murdered by the ship's gunnery officer.

A couple of women sailed as engineer officers, the most remarkable being Victoria Drummond, who overcame prejudice and deliberate obstruction to become the first woman marine engineer in Britain. During the war she served on a number of foreign vessels – the British government refused to allow her to serve in the Merchant Navy even though she had done so in peacetime for many years – and when her vessel came under attack in 1940 her bravery and ingenuity saved it from being sunk. An officer who served with her described her as 'the most courageous woman I ever saw' and went on to say that she 'is very good at her job and has an uncanny power over engines, for which I once thanked God'.[20] In recognition of the courage she displayed when her ship was bombed by the Luftwaffe, she was awarded an MBE and a Lloyd's War Medal for Bravery.[21]

THE CONVOY SYSTEM

The British were reluctant to introduce the convoy system, which entailed ships travelling in groups protected by warships. Ship owners in particular were strongly opposed to the idea, arguing that it slowed down shipping as the convoy could only travel at the speed of the slowest vessel, whereas individual and unescorted ships could carry supplies faster to their destination. They claimed it was unnecessary as there were more merchant ships than submarines so sheer numbers would enable the supplies to get through.[22]

A more cynical view of their mindset is that when a ship was sunk by the enemy the owners collected the insurance money and so were indemnified against loss. They knew they would no longer have to pay the wages of the merchant seamen and any ships sunk would need replacing, giving them the opportunity to make more money. Their attitude meant that merchant ships were unnecessarily vulnerable through travelling as single vessels, thereby providing easy targets for submarines. Eventually Churchill was forced to override the ship owners and insist on ships travelling in convoys.[23]

Merchant ship captains objected to a convoy's constraints on freedom of movement and resented the additional workload and security measures it required them to follow. Watches on ships had to be doubled and with scarce manpower that meant longer hours on duty and less sleep. The captains felt that with so many merchant ships travelling slowly it was safer for the vessels to sail independently and provide the U-boats with a single target than have a group of ships clustered together.[24]

Even the Navy was not happy about carrying out escort duties. The Admiralty remained mesmerized by the notion of a latter-day Battle of Trafalgar in which the German surface fleet would confront the British, so they resented sending warships on guard duty and considered it beneath their dignity.[25]

More rational objections were made by some in the Admiralty. Most naval ships were designed for conflict with other surface vessels and so there was an acute shortage of ships suitable for convoy duty. An additional cause for concern was the fear of a German invasion, which led to fierce disputes between those who wished to retain the fleet in British waters for a possible defensive role and those who wanted it to sail on escort duties to protect trade. This fundamental disagreement was not finally resolved until the autumn of 1940, when British losses at sea became so heavy that Churchill was forced to side with the advocates of the convoy system. Even then it came at the expense of a desperate plea to Roosevelt for 50 antiquated American ships in return for 99-year leases for US bases in British territory.[26]

Ships took years to build and many of the vessels in the Navy had been constructed some years before. It was neither quick nor easy to replace them and in the eyes of the Admiralty it was better to retain them for home defence and for possible action against the German fleet than expose them to the dangers of destruction to protect merchant shipping.

The convoy system was voluntary at the start of the war. It was not made compulsory for some time and in practice it would have been impossible to make it so at that stage. There were too few vessels available for escort duty and with both the Royal and the Merchant Navy hostile to the system, compulsion would not have been successful.

On 6 September 1939 the first British convoy sailed from the Thames to the Forth and a week later five other convoy routes were created. All were designed to protect ships travelling at a speed of 9 to 15 knots (10–17 mph). Faster or slower vessels had to sail independently and unprotected. There were so few ships available for escort duty that the convoys could only be escorted up to 200 miles (320 km) west of Ireland or beyond Ushant in the Bay of Biscay. Once the escorts reached these boundary points the merchant ships were abandoned and made their own way to and from their destination.[27]

BRITISH MEASURES TO STRENGTHEN THE NAVY AND COMBAT SUBMARINES

The Royal Navy's size and strength was primarily useful in direct confrontation with other surface vessels and for the first three years of the war it was ineffective against U-boats. One reason was a shortage of ships. Britain now possessed less than half as many destroyers as it had done in the First World War. Large capital ships took time and money to build and emphasis was placed on constructing new ships that could be built rapidly.

The most important was the corvette class, a small escort vessel that took 12 months to build rather than years.[28] Later, an improved version of the corvette known as the frigate was commissioned.[29]

The *Flower* class corvettes were the workhorses of escort duty in the Battle of the Atlantic. Cheap and quick to build, they were uncomfortable and rolled to an extreme degree in rough weather, but this tendency to pitch and toss enabled them to ride out the stormiest seas. And though they were despised by the crews of battleships their sailors were hardy and resourceful, enduring cramped conditions, humidity and poor ventilation. There was a shared camaraderie among corvette crews and none of the class distinction between officers and men that was so prevalent on more 'glamorous' naval vessels. Most corvette crews lived on dried or canned food with fresh food lasting no longer than three days and to protect themselves against the cold the sailors drank cocoa boiled in water.[30]

The corvettes struggled against fierce winds and the onrushing waves were at times powerful enough to bend iron bars. Lifeboats were sometimes smashed to pieces by the force of the waves and metal furniture welded to the deck could be ripped away and washed into the ocean. Ice created greater difficulties, with everything from gun emplacements to the ship's deck frozen solid. In this situation the crew chiselled away at the ice for hours and wore gloves before touching any item. Corvette crews learned to adapt to the most extreme conditions and these small ships became the backbone of the escort vessels during the war.[31]

Merchant ships were increasingly armed and asked to perform escort duties for other ships. This meant that from the point of international maritime law they were no longer civilian vessels but armed merchantmen and could be sunk without warning. However, the shortage of destroyers meant the British preferred to take the risk and husband their scarce resources of warships.

So great was the need for new ships to be built that British shipyards were unable to cope. Yards in Canada were then pressed into service, but even this failed to meet demand.[32] The French worked hard to complete their battleships, the *Richelieu* and the *Jean Bart*, against the growing threat of Italian intervention in the war.[33]

Aircraft carriers were used to protect vulnerable ships sailing towards British waters but this strategy proved costly, with the prized *Ark Royal* being attacked by a U-boat on 14 September. A few days later the carrier *Courageous* was sunk, with considerable loss of life. Air cover could be given when ships began their departure from British ports but this coverage could not extend far into the Atlantic, owing to shortage of range and the necessity to preserve aircraft for home defence.

Under a treaty between the British and the Irish governments signed in 1938, Britain gave up its naval bases in Ireland. A direct appeal by Chamberlain to the Irish leader Éamon de Valera to allow Britain to use them in the changed situation met with a flat refusal. When Churchill suggested to Chamberlain that Britain should occupy the ports by force, his idea was overruled and throughout the war the former Irish bases remained closed to British ships. Even when Churchill became prime minister and bluntly proposed handing over Northern Ireland to the Irish in exchange for the naval bases, de Valera refused his offer.[34]

THE GROWING PROBLEMS WITH SUPPLYING BRITAIN

The bravery of the crews of the corvettes and other ships and the growing implementation of the convoy system did not stop the enemy exacting a relentless toll on merchant shipping. Between September 1939 and March 1940 a total of 581 ships were sunk and 2.3 million tons (2.1 million tonnes) of goods were lost. Food imports dropped by a third and in March 1940 meat rationing was introduced.

Churchill recognized the danger of food shortages and ordered 40,000 additional workers to be recruited to build and repair ships. Unfortunately, this directive had little effect as skilled workers took time to train and there was profound hostility between shipyard workers and the Controller of Merchant

British seamen are rescued from their raft after a U-boat attack on a North Atlantic convoy, May 1940.

Shipbuilding and Repair, Sir James Lithgow. Lithgow had clashed with trade unions before the war, laying off thousands of workers and closing down shipyards.

This 'history' between him and the men was bad enough but Lithgow pursued a short-sighted policy in his government role. He opposed measures of standardization, centralized control and expanding production. Ernest Bevin, Churchill's Minister of Labour, tried to mediate but was unable to improve the relationship between Lithgow and the workers or significantly affect the rate of production of new ships. The result was a shortage of vessels to replace the ships being sunk, to the extent that Churchill became convinced that without American support Britain would lose the Battle of the Atlantic. However, the 50 antiquated US destroyers were a sticking plaster rather than a solution.[35]

TECHNICAL DEVELOPMENTS

Hydrophones were the main detection system used by U-boats. They consisted of two pairs of underwater microphones that picked up the sound of a ship's propeller. The hydrophone worked out the distance between the U-boat and the detected vessel and was capable of detecting convoys over 60 miles (100 km) away.[36]

In 1941, one of the best weapons available to the Allies was introduced, with ships and aircraft being fitted with short-wave radar sets capable of detecting U-boats on the surface. An improved version of ASDIC also improved detection rates.[37]

High-Frequency Direction Finding (HF/DF – nicknamed Huff-Duff), which allowed an operator to trace the direction of a radio signal, was fitted to escort ships. As the U-boats signalled to one another by radio this enabled more of their messages to be picked up and the approximate location of the submarines could be detected. Once the direction was identified a naval destroyer attacked the U-boat or drove it to submerge again.

Two escort vessels equipped with HF/DF could determine the position as well as the direction of the U-boat and this system greatly reduced the number of successful attacks on convoys.

HF/DF was not known to the Germans, who imagined that the British, like themselves, were still using pre-war technology that consisted of a manual aerial rotated to fix the direction of the transmitter. It led to the Germans imagining that if they kept radio messages short they would be immune from detection. This error resulted in a dramatic fall in successful U-boat attacks on shipping. HF/DF and radar made it easier for convoys to detect hostile submarines before they could launch an assault, so these technical developments turned the balance of battle. In early 1943, the situation for the Allies was so critical that it appeared the war at sea was lost, but by May Dönitz was forced to admit that he had been decisively defeated in the Battle of the Atlantic.[38]

The Germans eventually recognized that the British were using a new method, though they never identified Huff-Duff itself. In August 1944 they began developing the Kurier system, which could transmit an entire signal in a burst no longer than 454 milliseconds, making it too short to be located or decrypted. However, it was still at the development stage when the war ended. Whether it would have made a significant difference to the course of the naval battle remains uncertain.[39]

RADAR TO THE RESCUE
Both sides employed a variety of detection devices including early forms of radar and the Germans countered British radar systems by fitting U-boats with a device known as the Metox 600, which could detect radar transmitters in approaching aircraft before they became visible, thus making radar useless as a detection system.

An Allied tanker is torpedoed in the Atlantic by a U-boat, 1942. The vessel curled amidships under heat of fire, then sank.

In the spring of 1943 a radically new form of radar was developed, which operated on a 10 cm (4 in) wavelength with a range of up to 60 miles (96 km). The new radar system could detect the conning tower of a U-boat from a distance of 12 miles (19 km) and most importantly it could not be detected by the Metox 600 device.

The result of this new and more sophisticated radar development was to dramatically reduce the number of ships sunk by German submarines. It also enabled the Allies to detect and destroy U-boats at a faster rate. The Germans, while initially perplexed, developed the Naxos radar detector which was capable of detecting 10 cm radar wavelengths, but its range was short and in the event of detection the U-boat had little time to take evasive action. The combination of adequate air cover and the new advanced radar system still turned the tide, in spite of German ingenuity.[40] The changing fortunes of war now meant that for the first time in the conflict at sea the hunters were now the hunted.

BREAKING THE CODE

Codebreakers on both sides of the conflict contributed to the course of the naval war. The Germans had a head start in the process after they successfully cracked the British naval code during the Spanish Civil War.[41] However, the British success in breaking the German 'Enigma' code is better known. The codebreakers took advantage of the fact that Dönitz required continual radio communication between U-boats and naval headquarters, which enabled the messages to be detected by the British. For a long time, the Enigma cipher machine was considered unbreakable and even the personnel at Bletchley Park, when asked to decipher the encrypted messages, initially considered it impossible.

Enigma was originally designed in the 1920s for commercial use and when Poland was conquered by the Nazis the efforts of Polish codebreakers were passed on and provided a head start for the people at Bletchley Park. When a key was pressed on the Enigma machine keyboard a cipher-text lamp displaying a different letter lit up. This was further complicated by passing the electrical circuit that connected the keys and the lamps through a series of rotors, which made the circuit change at each keystroke. There was also a plugboard connected to the machine into which ten pairs of letters were entered each day, thereby adding a further layer of obfuscation.

Some success in deciphering the codes followed, but as there had been a number of improvements it was only possible to read a few of the German signals.

The consensus among cryptographers was that Enigma was not going to yield anything further, but the mathematician Alan Turing disagreed and set to work attempting to break the code. Turing had devised what became known as the Bombe in September 1939, a machine designed to decrypt the German cipher. The machines themselves, which weighed a ton, were built by the British Tabulating Machine Company (BTM) under the codename CANTAB. They contained the equivalent of 36 Enigma machines. It had been discovered that many German messages contained standard phrases, which were dubbed 'cribs'. This enabled the original and coded version of each of the letters in that part of the message to be deduced. The Bombe was rewired using that information and it then searched every possible rotor starting position until a match was found, at which point the Bombe stopped. After copying the rotor settings from the stopped Bombe, the codebreakers could eventually deduce that day's key and set up an Enigma machine that would mimic those used by the Germans.

Mathematician Alan Turing set to work to build on the foundations laid by Polish codebreakers to crack the Enigma code.

A stroke of good fortune came when *U-33* was destroyed in February 1940. Before the boat was abandoned the Navy managed to capture three Enigma rotors and this enabled the British to know the wiring of the machine. Then in early 1941 *U-110* was captured by the Royal Navy and the vessel's entire code and cipher material was recovered. This enabled the progress of U-boats to be followed for several weeks, but then the keys were changed. The codebreaking team then used its new familiarity with Enigma as a means of cracking the new codes, for example correctly predicting where the Italian fleet would be.[42]

This was strikingly successful at first and led to a marked decline in the sinking of Allied ships, but the problem resurfaced when a new Enigma network was created using a four-rotor, rather than a three-rotor, machine in February 1942. The new code could not be read by the Allied codebreakers and the result was a series of devastating raids on convoys by U-boat crews. For ten months this situation continued and although partial success in decryption was achieved by the team at Bletchley it was not enough to prevent the continuing assault on Allied shipping. HF/DF fixes on U-boat positions and such decryptions as could be achieved from messages using the earlier Enigma system were the best they could do when it came to tracking U-boat activity.[43]

It was not until good fortune came to the assistance of the Allies on 30 October 1942 that the problem was overcome. On that day *U-559* foundered near Port Said in Egypt and a British crew managed to obtain information about the new Enigma system from the wrecked submarine. Alan Turing and his team worked hard to break the code on the basis of the material they recovered and by December 1942 they had succeeded. Once more they could detect the position of U-boats and the result was a dramatic decline in shipping losses.[44]

By the end of the war there were 210 Bombe machines in operation. They were mainly operated by members of the Women's Royal Naval Service (WRENS) and by 1945 over 2,600 Wrens were involved in the task. These and other methods of cryptanalysis made a crucial difference to the British and, later, Allied war effort.[45]

On the other hand, the Germans continued to be able to decipher the British naval codes and that remained true throughout the war. They could always estimate when and where convoys were likely to occur. This knowledge meant that though success became more difficult U-boats continued to read naval signals and attack and destroy Allied shipping.[46] Curiously, both sides seemed to find it difficult to accept that their code had been broken. Dönitz raised the possibility with his naval superiors and from 1943 onwards with the leading Nazis, but his suspicions were consistently dismissed. It was flatly asserted that Enigma was unbreakable and there must be other explanations for the Allied success in detecting German submarines.

The British were even more dismissive of the idea that the Germans had cracked their naval cipher and not until the war had ended did they discover how mistaken their complacency had been. This negligence meant that many lives were lost unnecessarily.

U-BOAT BASES AND BUNKERS

Before the war it was standard practice for U-boats to be refuelled at sea. The conquest of France and Norway allowed ports in those countries to be used as U-boat bases – sometimes known as submarine pens – which transformed their potential to attack British shipping. It also gave the Nazis a fresh pool of labour with which to construct bunkers for their boats. Each one needed around 15,000 workers to build it.

The constructors worked 24 hours a day in two 12-hour shifts. Materials such as cement and reinforced steel were initially transported from Germany but increasingly local materials were used. Before the war the main protective bases for submarines had been open-sided shelters with wooden foundations, but these became inadequate with the development of heavy bombers and in the 1930s the Naval Construction Office in Berlin examined alternatives. Two bunkers were built in Hamburg and Heligoland but the conquest of France enabled construction on sites facing the Atlantic coast.

The Allies bombed the bunkers from the beginning in an attempt to prevent them from being completed. Disrupting the supply of material, both through raids and deliberate sabotage, hindered the project and mechanical failure, particularly that of concrete pumps, was an additional problem during construction work on the bunkers.

The building of the bunkers was a vast and complex operation requiring the construction of wet and dry docks in covered bombproof bays, lock gates to guard the entrances and exits, offices, storage facilities, generators, machine shops, medical facilities, lavatories, ventilation systems, anti-aircraft weapons and water purification plants. Each base had to be designed as a self-contained freestanding dry dock in order to make it possible for maintenance and repairs to be carried out in between combat missions. It also had to be built to withstand aerial bombing, so concrete roofs were built with a reinforced thickness of up to 7 m (23 ft). The roofs were also protected by the construction of Fangrost screens, which consisted of two rows of concrete beams, each 2 m (6 ft 7 in) high and 1.5 m (5 ft) wide. The intention was to capture the bombs and explode them before they hit the main roof. One of their nicknames was 'bomb traps'.

There were four main types of bunker: the covered lock which was built over an existing lock; the construction bunker which was used to build new U-boats; fitting-out bunkers, in which U-boats were equipped after launch; and operational and repair bunkers. This last type was the most common and there were two variants. One was built on dry land, which meant moving U-boats into position on ramps, while the other was built across the water. When the water was pumped out it was then possible for repairs to be carried out in a dry dock.[47]

MINES

Weather, aircraft, ships and submarines were the main agents of death and destruction but mines accounted for a number of sinkings, particularly in the early stages of the war. The first casualty was the Dutch passenger liner *Simon Bolivar*, which was sunk on 18 November 1939 with 87 people killed. Three days later the British ship *Gipsy* hit a mine and the vessel was rocked by an explosion. There were few survivors. The same day saw the sinking of the Japanese liner *Terukuni Maru*. On this occasion the passengers and crew of the ship were all rescued.[48]

By the end of November almost 800 mines had been laid and the press raged against the 'latest abomination of German savagery', calling it 'bloody murder' and 'not war at all'.[49] The general public was more resigned to the situation with Mass Observation, a social studies project, reporting that they had 'not noticed any symptoms of shock over Hitler's new secret weapon – these things appear to be cynically accepted'.[50]

The new magnetic mines created havoc among shipping. It was only when one was caught in the mud of the Thames Estuary and retrieved by a team of experts that its secrets were unlocked. The mine was defused on 23 November and its discovery came just in time. November alone saw 27 ships sunk and the Thames Estuary was temporarily closed to shipping.

In 1940 the 20th Destroyer Flotilla was attempting to intercept a German convoy when it hit a German minefield off the coast of Holland. Two destroyers were sunk and a third was severely damaged. There were 400 casualties in all.[51]

By March 1940 mines laid off British waters had accounted for the loss of 430,000 tons of shipping. They were second only to U-boats in terms of their destructive effect. The greater use of minesweepers and fitting degaussing systems (electrical cables surrounding a ship's hull, which cancelled out the vessel's magnetic field) made magnetic mines less effective. Conventional mines continued to be a hazard to shipping and caused the destruction of four merchant ships off the coast of England during October and November 1939. Throughout the war mines sank ships and submarines on both sides of the conflict.[52]

The British then joined in by laying mines in the Straits of Dover to discourage U-boats. Three ships were lost to mines in October and after that the Germans avoided the English Channel and sailed around the north of Scotland to reach the Atlantic Ocean.[53]

MIDGET SUBMARINES

Midget submarines were employed as well as U-boats. These were small one- or two-man submarines with their own propulsion system. They had no sleeping or even toilet facilities as all of the space was taken up by a cockpit from which the pilot launched the torpedo fitted beneath the boat, hence their nickname 'human torpedoes'. Midget submarines were only capable of short missions but because of their small size they were harder to detect than standard U-boats. They were also more resistant to depth charges, because of their light weight.

However, they lacked firepower and had limited endurance, with little in the way of life support systems. In addition, seasickness and carbon monoxide were constant problems for the crew. Very few midget submarines were produced and many pilots died of suffocation rather than enemy action. Out of 79 'human torpedoes' launched in 1943 only 12 survived. It was one of the most dangerous ways of attacking the enemy and verged on a suicide mission.[54]

LIVING CONDITIONS

The war at sea involved constant battles against the weather and demanded vigilance in order to spot the approach of aircraft, submarines and surface vessels. It tested courage, endurance and adaptability to the limit.

Life on tramp steamers was tough and the merchant seamen who sailed on them endured poor food, extreme weather and the high probability of being attacked. It was a test of character as much as seamanship to come through the ordeal. Few ships had refrigeration on board and the only frozen food came from an ice-box. Once the ice melted, the main diet was tinned butter and meat that was heavily salted from being kept in tubs of brine. Fresh fruit and vegetables was a rarity as was a supply of eggs. The ships were under strict instructions to cut costs to the bone and reducing the sailors' rations was the easiest route to achieving that.

Supper was generally cold ham and a slice of bread and butter. In theory, sailors were issued with a pound (450 g) of meat, a pound of bread and a pound of potatoes per day, along with 3 ounces (85 g) of tea, 3 ounces of coffee and 3 ounces of pickles. Eggs were supposed to be issued for breakfast twice a week. But in reality hardly any of these rations were issued to the men, apart from the tea, coffee and pickles.

Another trick was to make sure the cargo weighed less than 500 tons (454 tonnes). If it was over that weight, the ship owners were required to pay the crew an extra pound a month. In spite of the enormous dangers and unpleasant conditions under which merchant seamen operated during the war, their employers showed no respect for all the dedication and sacrifice. The sailors lived in confined spaces that were damp, dark, poorly ventilated and frequently rusty and slept in wooden bunks stacked three or more high. Running water and heating were rarely available. Only one or two blankets were provided and sometimes not even that amount of bed linen. The sailors were expected to bring their own mattress – a sackcloth bag stuffed with straw, which was nicknamed the 'donkey's breakfast' by the crew.[55]

Bad as the conditions on merchant ships were, life on a U-boat was worse. Crews might spend up to six months at sea, much of the time submerged beneath the waves. They were unable to bathe, shave or even change their clothes, fresh bread had to be eaten immediately or it became inedible and provisions were stored in every available space in the boat, including one of the boat's two lavatories. Using these was unpleasant and difficult, with up to 40 men having to share one of them for most of the journey. Waste matter was pumped out into the ocean, but this exposed the crew to danger as the operation could alert enemy ships or aircraft to the presence of a U-boat.

Each member of the crew had a locker for their personal belongings and the men's quarters doubled as the forward torpedo room. As one crew member left his bunk another member would often take his place. Sleep was difficult, as crews were kept half-awake by storms and anxiety about aircraft or ships seeking to detect the submarine. Crew members had no blankets or sheets but slept in sleeping bags. These were only washed on the crew's return to shore.

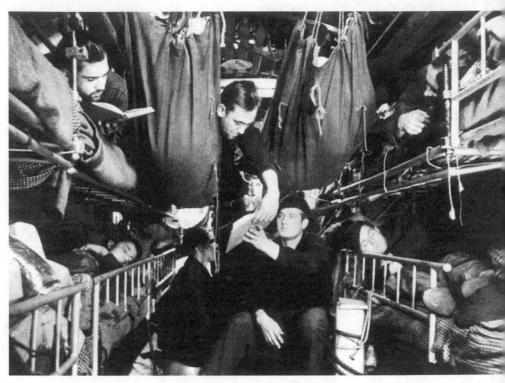

U-boat crew members off duty in their bunks, 1943. Life aboard a U-boat was cramped and unhygienic, and there was no privacy at all. But far worse was the fear of being discovered by a surface ship or plane or anything that could turn the sub into a watery grave.

Space was at a premium as U-boats were heavily armed with deck guns as well as torpedoes. The gangway on a submarine was only 2 ft (0.6 m) wide and conditions on board were cramped. Added to that, crews had only the clothes on their back and one change of underwear and socks. Saltwater soap was issued to remove excess salt from the skin, but it left an unpleasant film behind and deodorant and cologne were used to minimize the inevitable effects of body odour.

Seasickness affected not only sailors in surface ships but also submariners. However, U-boat crews were never seasick when submerged and there was one particular stretch of water south of Greenland where thanks to the area's currents even the crews of submarines travelling on the surface did not become seasick.

Smoking was forbidden on any part of a U-boat except on the deck when the submarine was surfaced. The result was that on long voyages in rough weather there was often a surplus of cigarettes. Fear was an ever-present reality but it was essential to disguise it. A brave front was maintained as any display of fear risked creating panic and lowering morale. The captains of U-boats were generally respected but were not on the whole authoritarian as the crew had to work as a team and there was none of the sharp distinction between officers and men so typical of most British ships.

One of the more bizarre aspects of U-boats was the way in which radio transmission was possible when a submarine was underwater. Condoms were used to raise wireless aerials with four condoms being used and filled with gas. They were also used to launch weather balloons.[56]

Harald Busch described some aspects of life on a U-boat:

> *The most striking thing when one is at sea for the first*
> *time on a war-experienced submarine is the sober*

realization of the difficulty of everyday life on board: flight alarms, submarine traps, pursuing destroyers, even torpedoes, weeks of bitter cold temperatures, and ongoing high seas. So many extreme efforts have to be made before a brief and simple war report can be dispatched mentioning even the most modest of successes. It's difficult to conceive of the effort behind such a report.[57]

Even survivors of the conflict at sea endured incredible hardships. Survivors of a U-boat attack had to take to the lifeboats and paddle through a sea that was rapidly filling with oil from the sinking ship. They could then drift on the open sea for days and sometimes weeks. If the vessel was on fire, escape was even more difficult and dangerous.

The type of cargo being carried made a huge difference to the chances of survival for the crew. Food or similar material would sink slowly and give the crew a greater chance of escape while military items like aircraft, tanks or weapons were heavy and would drag the ship down in a few minutes. The same was true of other heavy cargoes, like coal or iron.

But the most dangerous situation of all was when a ship was transporting oil or fuel. The torpedo from the U-boat would frequently burst the tanks, releasing a huge amount of heat and the fuel, combusting with the ocean air, would explode and create giant balls of fire.

To add insult to injury, merchant seamen who escaped from a sinking ship and made their way on to lifeboats would only be paid for the time they were serving on the ship. Time spent in the lifeboat was unpaid.

U-boat crews whose boat was sunk were often murdered in cold blood. It was even more common for them to be simply abandoned to their fate in the water by the crews of the warships or planes that had sunk them. Even those who were picked up were often manhandled by angry sailors.

NOTES

1   Padfield, *War Beneath the Sea*
2   Robert Hutchinson, *Jane's Submarines: War Beneath the Waves from 1776 to the Present Day*, Harper Collins, 2001
3   Padfield, *War Beneath the Sea*
4   http://www.german-navy.de/kriegsmarine/articles/feature4.html/
5   Frischauer and Jackson, op. cit.
6   T.K. Derry and J.R.M. Butler, *The Campaign in Norway: History of the Second World War*, United Kingdom Military Series, HMSO, 1952
7   Donald G.F.W. Macintyre, *Narvik*, W.W. Norton, 1959
8   Ibid.
9   Derry and Butler, op. cit.
10 Ibid.
11 Ibid.
12 Ibid.
13 Dimbleby, op. cit.
14 Ibid.
15 Ibid.
16 Padfield, *War Beneath the Sea*
17 Ibid.
18 Captain Jack Broome, *The Convoy is to Scatter*, William Kimber, 1972
19 Rear Admiral Sir Kenelm Creighton, *Convoy Commodore*, Futura, 1976
20 Cherry Drummond, *The Remarkable Life of Victoria Drummond – Marine Engineer*, Institute of Marine Engineers, 1994
21 Ibid.
22 Dimbleby, op. cit.
23 Ibid.
24 Ibid.
25 Ibid.
26 Ibid.
27 David Fairbank White, *Bitter Ocean: The Dramatic Story of the Battle of the Atlantic 1939–1945*, Headline, 2006
28 John Keegan, *The Price of Admiralty*, Viking, 1989

29 Norman Friedman, *British Destroyers and Frigates: The Second World War and After*, Greenhill Books, 2006

30 John Lambert and Les Brown, *Flower Class Corvettes*, Seaforth Publishing, 2010

31 Keegan, op. cit.

32 http://shipbuildinghistory.com/canadayards/redfern.htm

33 John Jordan and Robert Dumas, *French Battleships 1922–1956*, Seaforth Publishing, 2009

34 The Earl of Longford and Thomas P. O'Neill, *Éamon de Valera*, Arrow, 1974

35 Dimbleby, op. cit.

36 http://www.uboataces.com/hydrophones.shtml

37 Padfield, *War Beneath the Sea*

38 Ibid.

39 http://www.ticomarchive.com/iv-case-studies/kurier

40 Louis Brown, *A Radar History of World War II*, Institute of Physics Publishing, 1999

41 Antony Beevor, *The Battle for Spain: The Spanish Civil War 1936–1939*, Phoenix, 2006

42 E.H. Hinsley and Alan Stripp, *Code Breakers: The Inside Story of Bletchley Park*, Oxford University Press, 2001

43 Ibid.

44 Ibid.

45 Ibid.

46 Jak P. Mallmann Showell, *German Naval Codebreakers*, Naval Institute Press, 2003

47 Jak P. Mallmann Showell, *Hitler's U-boat Bases*, Sutton Publishing, 2002

48 Norman E. Youngblood, *The Development of Mine Warfare: A Most Murderous and Barbarous Conduct*, Praeger, 2006

49 Terry Charman, *Outbreak 1939: The World Goes to War*, Virgin, 2009

50 Ibid.

51 Youngblood, op. cit.

52 Ibid.

53 Ibid.

54 Padfield, *War Beneath the Sea*

55 Bill Linskey, *No Longer Required*, Pisces Press, 1999

56 https://www.uboataces.com/articles-life-uboat.shtml

57 Harald Busch, *Jagd im Atlantik*, C. Bertelsmann, 1943

CHAPTER FOUR

THE BATTLE OF THE ATLANTIC – FIRST PHASE

In the Atlantic Ocean ships rode out ferocious storms with waves so powerful that they ripped away iron fixtures, lashed the crew with wind and rain and even wrecked their ships. Frequent bouts of fog added to the difficulties of navigating the ocean. Many vessels could not cope with the conditions and air cover was not routinely provided until early 1943, which made attacks by U-boats, surface ships and occasionally the Luftwaffe easier and more deadly.[1]

Submarine crews endured equally difficult and dangerous conditions. Freezing waves rushed over the conning tower of the U-boat, submerging the boat and its crew, and men on watch had to be fastened by safety lines to prevent them from being washed into the sea. There were special coats for these conditions but they did not keep the men dry and there was no real possibility of drying their clothes when out on patrol. On top of that, fresh water was scarce and only permitted for drinking and even then it was rationed.

On 5 March 1941 the First Lord of the Admiralty, A.V. Alexander, requested 'many more ships and great numbers of

A depth charge is launched from US Coast Guard cutter Spencer. *In this engagement, German submarine U-175 was sunk and was therefore prevented from breaking into the centre of a large American convoy where it might have done a great deal of damage, 17 April 1943.*

men' to fight 'the Battle of the Atlantic'. Alexander did not originate the term but he was the first to use it in an official capacity and it caught the popular imagination.[2] On 19 March 1941 the 'Battle of the Atlantic Committee' met to make preparations for the long naval war.

GERMAN U-BOAT STRATEGY IN THE BATTLE OF THE ATLANTIC

Dönitz had little time for what he considered an old-fashioned approach to warfare. He saw using U-boats to attack the Royal Navy as a fundamentally mistaken strategy. Britain relied heavily on imports and he believed that the key to successful naval warfare was attacking merchant ships. He was convinced that with enough submarines he could stifle the flow of goods to Britain and force it to surrender.

Dönitz commanded the best submarine fleet in the world and his principal problem was a shortage of U-boats. A subsidiary, and serious, defect was revealed during the Norwegian campaign when torpedoes failed to explode, but this problem was swiftly corrected.

In spite of the heavy losses the German surface fleet had suffered in Norway and the poor performance of his submarines, Dönitz was confident that his U-boats could still deliver victory. The sudden availability of French ports for deployment meant that, as he wrote in his *Memoirs*, 'we should have an exit from our backyard'. Instead of sailing from German bases through the North Sea and around Scotland it was possible to use French harbours to attack shipping in the Atlantic.

Dönitz chose Lorient in the Bay of Biscay as his new HQ and by the end of June 1940 he began moving his U-boats to the new base. Some of his young commanders expected the war to end rapidly, even before they had been engaged in active combat.

Dönitz rebuked them sternly, saying: 'Don't forget that we're fighting the strongest sea power in the world!'[3]

BRITISH PROBLEMS

Dönitz's caution was understandable but Churchill was aware how stretched British naval resources were. As well as U-boats, two pocket battleships and other armed merchantmen posed a serious threat to British supplies. Although he ordered that the convoy system should become normal practice, the shortage of vessels to protect the merchant ships remained a problem.

The dearth of escort ships led to Churchill making a deal with Roosevelt whereby British territories were leased to the US as naval and air bases in return for 50 American destroyers that had been earmarked to be scrapped.[4] Unfair and one-sided as the arrangement was, these antiquated ships were a precious lifeline for Britain. Ships were being sunk at a rate that could not continue. The Royal Navy resisted the only practical alternative, which was to release Navy warships from the defence of home waters to the task of escorting convoys.

Operation Sea Lion, Hitler's plan to invade Britain, was a live option at the time, with over 1,000 barges and ships massing on the French side of the Channel and the Luftwaffe continuing to inflict heavy losses on the RAF. In the circumstances the Navy's excessively defensive strategy is more understandable.

THE SINKING OF THE *CITY OF BENARES*

Another tragedy helped increase American sympathy for Britain and led to growing revulsion against the Germans. In September 1940 a passenger liner, the *City of Benares*, sailed from Liverpool en route for Canada, carrying children who were being evacuated to Quebec. It was a civilian ship rather than a merchantman or a naval vessel and the passengers assumed they would be safe, with both sides being committed to observing the prize rules laid down under international maritime law.

The Children's Overseas Reception Board (CORB) organized the evacuation in response to public anger about the fact that wealthy parents were sending their children abroad while poorer families could not take advantage of that option. There were 90 children on the *City of Benares*, which was part of convoy OB-213, all of whom were sailing overseas in the expectation of a better, or at least safer, life away from the war.[5]

The ship sailed on 13 September 1940 and was spotted by *U-48* on the evening of 17 September. Kapitänleutnant Heinrich Bleichrodt, the U-boat's commander, fired three torpedoes at the ship but the first two missed. It had passed midnight on 18 September when the third torpedo was launched and struck the stern of the ship. The *City of Benares* sank half an hour after being hit.

The vessel was abandoned within 15 minutes of being torpedoed and there were problems with lowering the lifeboats. A day later HMS *Hurricane* discovered 105 survivors and took them back to Scotland.

An account by Bess Walder, a 15-year-old survivor of the attack, gives a vivid picture of their ordeal.

> *We fell asleep about half past eleven when we were literally shaken out of our beds by the explosion in the engine room where the U-boat torpedo had cleaved the power engine in two.*
>
> *This was followed by louder and terrifying detonations. I jumped up and put on my dressing gown, and fumbled for my life jacket (as we were completely in the dark as the lights went out) and*

grabbed hold of my mac. Then I fished the other two that were in my cabin, got their lifebelts and got one little girl out on to the boat deck. Then I went back for the other little girl Ailsa. I found that our wardrobe had blocked the cabin door. I grabbed hold of something and hacked at the wardrobe. I managed to squeeze through a hole and when I got there, into our cabin I found that Ailsa had fallen over something and was bleeding to death. I wrapped her in my coat that I wasn't wearing and tried to get out. The cabin was fast filling up with water and I found to my horror that I couldn't get past the wardrobe. Then I yelled and shouted and one of the escorts came along and managed to get us out. As we rushed along the passage, the stairs that led to our boat deck collapsed and so we had to rush along back again and use the other stairs. We got up these and just as we hopped up the last stair they commenced to collapse. We managed to hurry along to the lifeboat we were allotted and found that it had been smashed to smithereens.

The children were lowered into lifeboats but Bess's boat was overloaded and became waterlogged. Someone then had to put the children off the boat to see if the water could be baled out but huge waves made their task impossible. Out of the 70 people who had boarded the lifeboats only 20 were still alive. At that point the lifeboat capsized completely and Bess decided to swim to the upturned craft. On trying to get to it she discovered she had sprained her ankle but using her arms and one leg she was able to right the boat. At that point her friend Beth Cummins tried to get on and Bess helped her on board. They clung to the keel all night and in the morning they saw that no one else was in sight and they were surrounded on all sides by the Atlantic Ocean.

> *We drifted on the waves northwards (we could see huge fish and lumps of ice in the water) for about three and a half hours longer, wet through and through and now so numb that we couldn't feel our faces or our fingers. Then I fancied I saw something move on the horizon. I didn't tell Beth, as I didn't want to raise her hopes unduly. But then I saw some masts and as she drew nearer I saw the zigzag camouflage of a British Destroyer. The boat drew nearer, and then the sailors came to get us in a landing party boat.*[6]

Another ship, the *Marina*, was torpedoed during the attack and one of the lifeboats from that vessel was mistakenly assumed to be from the *City of Benares*. As a result the lifeboat drifted at sea, with three weeks' food provisions but only one week's supply of water. In that lifeboat were six boys, a number of sailors and a few civilians. They struggled in the waters of the Atlantic before an aircraft spotted them and they were rescued by HMS *Anthony*. Out of the 90 evacuees who had boarded the ships taking them to safety only 13 survived, while 134 passengers and 126 crewmen also perished.[7]

The tragedy led to the cancellation of the CORB programme to evacuate children abroad. Attempts by the organization to continue the scheme but with better protection were rejected and it was another example of how vulnerable ships were to attack by marauding U-boats.

This episode has generally been seen as an example of German ruthlessness but the truth is less simple and straightforward. The British failed to designate *City of Benares* as a Red Cross ship, which they could easily have done. It was the largest ship in the convoy and right in the centre so without any distinguishing markings the U-boat captain assumed it must be a merchant ship or a troopship. At this early stage of the war there was no way a U-boat would have intentionally sunk a passenger liner, still less one that should have been clearly marked as a Red Cross ship. Horrific though the ordeal of the passengers was, the tragedy was partly the result of British negligence.[8]

U-BOATS BEGIN TO ATTACK BRITISH CONVOYS

October 1940 saw the destruction of two British convoys, with results that made Churchill sense impending danger. He had quelled talk of peace a few months earlier and now the situation was extremely grave. Imports dropped dramatically as U-boats and, to a lesser extent, German surface raiders played havoc with British ships.[9]

CONVOY SC-7

On 5 October 1940 convoy SC-7 left Nova Scotia bound for Liverpool. It consisted of 35 merchant ships and a single escort, the sloop HMS *Scarborough*. At that stage it was not possible to provide long-range air cover and once the coastal area had been passed the ships were vulnerable to enemy aircraft.

The theoretical speed of the convoy was 8 knots per hour (9 mph), but as opponents of the convoy system pointed out many merchant ships could not attain this speed. Most of the vessels were old and slow and easy prey for a single U-boat and they were virtually defenceless against a wolfpack.

The convoy carried wood, steel, iron ore and fuel for the Royal Navy and a large consignment of trucks. Not all of the ships were British with Swedish, Dutch, Norwegian and Greek vessels joining the convoy. However, the multiple nationalities of the vessels hindered progress, with one Greek captain keeping his lights on at night which increased the danger to the convoy. Added to that, *Scarborough* had little capacity to fight off German U-boats.

On the first day of sailing one ship had to withdraw with mechanical problems and return to port. Then on 8 October a fierce gale blew up and a skirmish with German submarines took place. The weather worsened on 11 October and some of the slower ships lost contact with the main convoy. One of these stragglers, the Canadian ship *Trevisa*, carrying lumber intended for Scotland, was sighted by *U-124* on 16 October and sunk. Next day the Greek freighter *Aenos* was attacked and sunk by another U-boat, *U-38*. One Canadian ship, the *Eaglescliffe Hall*, evaded attack and managed to rescue survivors from the *Aenos*, reaching Scotland on 19 October and another ship that had become separated rejoined the convoy.

On 17 October the lone protector *Scarborough* was joined by two more vessels, the sloop *Fowey* and the corvette *Bluebell*, but they were unable to prevent *U-48* from attacking and sinking two ships. *Scarborough* attacked the raider and managed to drive it deep beneath the surface, but when the captain tried to pursue the submarine he lost contact with the convoy. On 18 October two more ships, the sloop *Leith* and the corvette *Heartsease*, joined the convoy but another U-boat then attacked them and damaged another merchant ship. This forced *Heartsease* to abandon the convoy and escort the damaged ship home alone. On 18 and 19 October five U-boats, *U-46*, *U-99*, *U-100*, *U-101* and *U-123*, attacked in a wolfpack. The *Creekirk*, carrying iron ore to Wales, was sunk with all 36 crew on board lost and later that night, during a six-hour attack, 15 more ships were sunk with considerable loss of life. Another ship, the *Blairspey*, was more fortunate, because it managed to remain afloat after being torpedoed twice by two different U-boats and was able to be towed to Scotland and repaired.

The escorts were unable to prevent the catastrophic losses and were both strategically and tactically naïve in their attempts to combat the U-boats. At no time did they realize that German submarines were attacking the ships from within the convoy rather than outside it or from a submerged position. They were on the surface and weaving in and out of the ships. Most of the escorts' time was spent rescuing survivors rather than combating the U-boats and an air of panic was compounded by chaos and failure to recognize the nature of the attack. It would still have been difficult to avoid loss of life, but the incompetence of the British merchant fleet contributed greatly to the disaster.

Out of the 35 ships that sailed on convoy SC-7, 20 were sunk and nearly 80,000 tons of shipping was lost, but not a single U-boat was lost or damaged. It was a triumph for the wolfpack strategy and a devastating blow to British supplies.[10]

CONVOY HX-79

The disaster was compounded by the arrival in the area of a second convoy, HX-79. This presented the U-boats with new targets and they proceeded to attack. The tragedy of SC-7 had alarmed the Admiralty and so they sent armed warships to protect the convoy. But the U-boats attacked under cover of darkness and approached the ships on the surface, attacking from within the convoy itself. Thirteen ships were torpedoed in all, out of which ten were sunk and two were lost. A further vessel was damaged but made its way to safety. Twelve out of the 49 ships in HX-79 were destroyed and a total tonnage of over 75,000 was lost, but no U-boats were sunk or damaged.

The result of these two convoy voyages was the loss of 32 ships, damage to others and a huge volume of tonnage sunk.

The episodes showed the lack of co-ordination between the protecting vessels and the ships in the convoy and the failure to realize that the U-boat attacks were not coming from outside but from within the convoys themselves. These huge losses represented the worst two days for merchant ships in the Battle of the Atlantic and the double tragedy led to the fundamental rethinking of escort duties by the Admiralty.[11]

The most important tactical change was creating escort groups. This meant that ships had to operate together under clear leadership and follow orders (which had not been the case in either of the two convoys sunk in the wolfpack attacks). The belated change of policy meant that convoys were better protected and better able to respond to U-boat attacks. A horrific level of casualties continued but at least there was a greater appreciation of some of the measures necessary to protect British shipping.

FLAWS IN BRITISH NAVAL STRATEGY

British dependence on imports was a key problem and the nation needed over a million tons of imports a week to survive. The necessity for trade to continue flowing was recognized but the difficulties in providing sufficient escort vessels for convoys, the reluctance of the Royal Navy to act as guards rather than fighting German shipping and the inability to replace vessels in sufficient quantities made the conduct of the war difficult.

These problems were compounded by Churchill's instructions to the Navy to seek out and destroy U-boats. The Royal Navy's anti-submarine groups were based on aircraft carriers which attempted to hunt them down, but a U-boat on the surface could quickly detect the warships and descend beneath the water. Aircraft carriers offered little assistance in the fight against U-boats as the planes lacked the offensive capability to attack a U-boat and sightings of a submarine by an aircraft were fruitless as the U-boat escaped before warships arrived on the scene.

An equally flawed strategy was the use of destroyers escorting convoys to pursue U-boats. Although they rarely detected submarines, they exposed the convoys to greater risk of attack. The continuing German success in sinking merchant ships led to the British reconsidering their strategy. They decided that fewer but larger convoys would result in greater protection for the ships than a greater number of small convoys. It allowed convoys to be assembled more quickly and yet carry the same amount of cargo. This realization reduced danger but the inability to replace ships quickly enough after sinking remained a problem and for the time being the U-boats were winning the naval war for Germany.

The Royal Navy had given little thought to combating submarines and believed U-boats would play only a peripheral role in a naval war. They relied on inshore patrol boats fitted with hydrophones and depth charges and for the first two years of the war continued to believe that ASDIC was a foolproof method of detecting submarines. Combating submarines was also seen as a purely defensive measure that lacked the 'glamour' of battles at sea between large surface vessels.

The Royal Navy also suffered from the preconception that the tactics employed by German submarines would be similar to those used during the First World War. During that conflict submarines had been largely coastal craft which had concentrated their efforts on attacking approaches to ports. This led the Navy to think that it would not be necessary to provide long-range escort support for convoys. There was a lack of training in anti-submarine warfare among naval officers and the use of U-boats as aggressors in the open sea caught them by surprise. Initially they had no idea of how to respond to the unexpected threat.

In addition, air cover was patchy and the aircraft available to RAF Coastal Command did not have the range to cover the Atlantic Ocean. When they saw a submarine diving, they could only attack it with machine-gun fire as they lacked the heavy armament required to sink a U-boat. The RAF gave priority to the Fighter and Bomber Commands so Coastal Command was not given the aircraft and equipment it needed, earning it the nickname 'Cinderella Service'. These factors rendered air cover, even when available, relatively ineffective.[12]

NEW NAVAL STRATEGY

Following the disasters that befell the two British convoys in October 1940 naval thinking was radically overhauled. The introduction of escorts as standard helped, as did the American destroyers and the new *Flower* class corvettes which Canada as well as Britain used to great effect. The Canadian navy expanded dramatically during the war, from a small fleet of destroyers to an imposing armada of warships. Also available to the British were ships belonging to the Free French forces and the Dutch and Norwegian resistance groups, but these comprised only a handful of the escort vessels.

Air cover, though still patchy, began to be provided more frequently. The result was not only greater protection for ships but the occasional success in sinking U-boats. On 12 December 1940, for instance, a U-boat was observed prowling in the Atlantic. On being spotted by British aircraft it immediately submerged but had only half completed the manoeuvre when it was hit on the front bow. It was bombed again and within a minute the stern rose and fell. An oil patch then spread out across the water and the outline of a submarine could be clearly distinguished within it. The U-boat was hit again and sank beneath the waves.

In the early stages of escorting convoys the protective groups were mainly two or three destroyers and five or six corvettes, with six vessels per convoy being the average. New training was provided to crews to deal with the threat of submarines and a base was set up in the Hebrides to make the ships and crew ready for the new type of naval warfare. February 1941 saw the headquarters of the Western Approaches Command moved to Liverpool. This enabled closer contact with the Atlantic convoys and helped control the flow of shipping. Aircraft were used more frequently in a supporting role and co-ordination between the RAF and the Royal Navy increased. In April that year Coastal Command planes came under the direct command of the Admiralty.

As early as the spring of 1941 these tactical changes had an effect on the naval war. An important sea battle took place between convoy HX-112 and a U-boat pack. The 5th Escort Group, comprising two corvettes and five destroyers, fought with the wolfpack and sank two U-boats. In the space of three weeks the three top submarine 'aces' were killed or captured. This dispirited the Germans and boosted British morale, while forcing Dönitz to adopt a different strategy. He moved his submarines further west, hoping to catch convoys coming from the other side of the Atlantic before the escorting ships were able to protect them.

The new deployment of the U-boat packs enabled an attack on convoy SC-26 before it had been joined by its escort and ten ships were sunk for the loss of one U-boat. Moving the area of operation to more thinly protected regions of the Atlantic led to renewed German success in the naval war, but before long the Allies took countermeasures.[13]

TRANSATLANTIC CONVOY PROTECTION

By June 1941 Britain realized that it was essential to provide convoys with escort ships for the entire passage of the North Atlantic. The Canadian navy was asked to protect ships in the western region and so they set up a base on Newfoundland. Six destroyers and 17 corvettes were provided and the Royal Navy contributed seven destroyers, three sloops and five corvettes. These escorts shepherded the convoys to Newfoundland and then Iceland, at which point the British ships took over escort duties.[14]

Roosevelt then pushed the boundaries of neutrality and in April 1941 declared that the Pan-American Security Zone would extend far to the east, almost to Iceland. When Denmark was conquered by the Germans the British occupied Iceland and used it as a base. The US then agreed that American troops could relieve the British forces on Iceland.[15]

American warships began escorting Allied convoys as far as Iceland and this led to clashes with German submarines. An incident on 21 May involving an American ship, the *Robin Moor*, which was stopped by *U-69* near Sierra Leone, helped harden American opinion. The ship carried no supplies of any military value – although this was initially disputed both by the Germans and by American isolationists – but the captain was given 30 minutes to evacuate the passengers and crew on to lifeboats before the U-boat sank the vessel. Survivors of the attack drifted on the ocean for 18 days without being rescued or discovered.[16] The sinking of the *Robin Moor* enraged and concerned American shipping companies and drew a stern editorial from *Time* magazine in June 1941, which stated that:

> *If such sinkings continue, U.S. ships bound for other places remote from fighting fronts will be in danger.*

Henceforth the U.S. would either have to recall its ships from the ocean or enforce its right to the free use of the seas.[17]

The decision by Roosevelt to escort British convoys up to Iceland was a gross violation of neutrality amounting to a declaration of war on Germany but Hitler, desperate to keep the United States out of the war and with the invasion of the Soviet Union his top priority, did not react. It led to a growing sense that the war was drawing closer to America and helped prepare the public for entry into the conflict later that year. Roosevelt was as conscious as the British of his resource problems and over-extended supply lines but continued to push the boundaries of neutrality in the hope of provoking the Germans into war.[18]

THE CAPTURE OF A U-BOAT

U-570 was on its maiden patrol on 27 August 1941 when it was spotted by two Hudson Coastal Command planes near Iceland. The first aircraft dived and released four depth charges which failed to hit the submarine and the U-boat dived rapidly before re-emerging on the surface. Then the pilot of the second Hudson shot at the submarine. Its pilot, Squadron Leader James Thompson, described the events that followed:

The sea was rough, and covered with angry white-caps. The clouds were low, and we kept on running into rain-storms and patches of dirty weather. We flew a good many miles close down to the sea – nothing to look at but clouds, and waves, and rain, and it was getting a bit monotonous.

The first thing I knew about the U-boat was a shout from my second pilot: 'There's one just in front of you.' When I came round again in a tight turn, the whole area of the sea was churned up into a foaming mass, and in the middle of it the U-boat suddenly popped to the surface again.

The pilot began shooting at the U-boat and as he was preparing for another assault the conning tower hatch was flung open. He saw men coming on to the deck and imagined they were about to counter-attack so he resumed firing. After four more circles of the boat the crew decided to surrender.

They stuck a white rag of some sort out of the conning-tower, and waved it violently. We found out afterwards that it was a shirt they were using for a white flag. [19]

After the crew had hoisted their white shirt as a signal of surrender the plane circled the U-boat and called for help. A Catalina aircraft and the armed trawler *Kingston Agate* arrived and the U-boat was captured and taken to Iceland. Neither codes nor secret documents were recovered but as it was the first example of a complete U-boat it was studied eagerly by British naval and scientific experts before being refitted and returned to service, this time as Royal Navy submarine *Graph*. Thompson, his navigator and his co-pilot all received the Distinguished Flying Cross for capturing the U-boat. It was one of the few triumphs for the Allies at this stage of the Battle of the Atlantic and it provided a welcome boost to morale, with the tide of battle still being in favour of the Germans at that stage.

MERCHANT SEAMEN CONTINUE TO SUFFER

All of these technical improvements, coupled with a greater degree of protection for merchant seamen, did not prevent horrific loss of life and the catastrophic destruction of cargo.

German U-boat, the U-570, which was captured in the Atlantic by a Hudson aircraft of the Coastal Command, comes into port under the White Ensign.

John Bradbury joined the Merchant Navy when he was 16 years old and when war broke out he soon found himself facing the U-boat menace. Initially he spent ten months sailing without incident but in 1943 he was sunk twice in one month. He describes his first sinking when he was on the ship *William Wilberforce*:

> *By 9th January, we were about 500 miles [800 km] west of the Canary Islands. At about 8pm, the ship was struck by 2 torpedoes on her starboard side. I was on the bridge with the chief officer and four others when it happened and being on the starboard side, I was knocked out by the explosion. Fortunately, the water pouring over me brought me round pretty quickly as within a few seconds the ship started to list and about 10 minutes later she sank.*
>
> *The starboard lifeboats had been blown away in the explosion, so the passengers and some of the crew boarded the two remaining lifeboats on the port side.*
>
> *A discovery was made quite early on that the emergency food rations stored in the lifeboat lockers were missing which was depressing. When daylight came we realised that three men were missing – presumably killed in the explosions or when the ship sank. It was on the fifth day that [we] were sighted by a Basque ship. Once he had picked us up he gallantly spent several hours searching for the second lifeboat until they too were rescued.*[20]

The crew were taken to Tenerife and repatriated to Gibraltar. Bradbury was then put on another ship, the *Mary Slessor*, but again disaster struck.

'Mary Slessor' hit a mine in the Straits that night and sank in 15 minutes. I found myself floating in a life jacket in the Atlantic again. 'Mary Slessor' had lost half her crew (including some of the survivors from the 'William Wilberforce') and her cargo of oranges and fuel oil was spread across the water around me. I was 'off' oranges for a very long time after that! The convoy sailing past had instructions not to pick up survivors and I was left bobbing up and down in the cold water shouting, 'you bastards!' as they went by. Some of us clung to an upturned lifeboat for about 3 hours before we were picked up by a Canadian ship and returned to Gibraltar.[21]

THE *GREER* INCIDENT

On 4 September 1941 the American destroyer *Greer* was sailing towards Iceland when an RAF bomber sent a signal to its captain. The message announced 'enemy U-boat observed submerging about ten miles (16 km) northwest'. The *Greer* proceeded to pursue the submarine, which took evasive action.

For three hours the warship stalked the U-boat until the RAF pilot asked if the ship intended to attack. Receiving a negative answer – the instructions to American ships were to observe U-boats but refrain from initiating an attack – the pilot dropped four depth charges from his plane. He then flew away to refuel his aircraft.

Not surprisingly, the U-boat captain assumed that the destroyer had fired its depth charges at him. He responded by firing a torpedo but the *Greer* sailed away from it. The *Greer* responded by launching depth charges and a second torpedo was fired from the submarine. This too was evaded by the

Greer but in doing so it lost sight of the submarine. It then spent nearly three hours searching for the U-boat before locating it once more and launching 11 further depth charges against it. All missed and the *Greer* lost contact with the U-boat so the captain was ordered to continue his journey to Iceland. It was the first encounter between an American warship and a German submarine. There were no casualties but Roosevelt seized on the incident as a propaganda weapon.[22]

On 11 September Roosevelt gave one of his 'Fireside Chats', in which he denounced the attack and was highly economical with the truth. He declared:

> *If the destroyer was visible to the submarine when the torpedo was fired, the attack was a deliberate attempt by the Nazis to sink a clearly identified American vessel. If the submarine was beneath the waves it indicates a policy of indiscriminate violence against any vessel sailing the seas.*

Roosevelt carefully avoided mentioning the depth charges dropped by the RAF pilot which had initiated the entire incident, claiming that the U-boat's purely defensive actions were 'piracy, legally and morally'. The president then resurrected the attack on the *Robin Moor* three months previously and claimed that the US needed 'to stop being deluded by the romantic notion that the Americas can go on living happily in a Nazi-dominated world'. The attack on the *Greer*, he declared, was 'one determined step towards creating a permanent world system based on force, on terror, and on murder'.[23]

Roosevelt was not content with massaging the truth about the encounter between the *Greer* and the U-boat. He went on to announce that 'if any German or Italian vessels of war enter the waters, the protection of which is necessary for American defense, they do so at their own peril'.[24] He was in fact instructing the US navy to shoot at Axis vessels in the North Atlantic, though he continued to avoid an open declaration of war.

CONSEQUENCES OF ROOSEVELT'S ACTIONS

The effect of Roosevelt's declaration was a considerable slowdown in German attacks in the North Atlantic. Hitler remained desperate to avoid American involvement in the war and gave strict orders to U-boats never to attack US vessels. From September to December 1941 there was a stalemate in that theatre of war, with the U-boats transferring their main focus of activity to the seas around Africa.

Following the relative quiet in the western reaches of the Atlantic Ocean, Hitler ordered Dönitz to move U-boats into the Mediterranean. Dönitz protested the decision to Raeder but he had to comply. The result was a series of naval battles in the Gibraltar region between convoys coming from Africa.

THE BATTLES AROUND GIBRALTAR

Holding Gibraltar was a strategic necessity for Britain, both to ensure that supplies to Malta continued and to prevent Axis forces from overrunning North Africa. Convoys sailing via Gibraltar to Britain received heavy protection by sea and air and attacking them was a prime objective of the Germans.

Convoy HG-73, comprising 25 ships and escorted by ten corvettes and destroyers, sailed from Gibraltar on 17 September, its destination being Milford Haven. Almost at once its departure was reported by German agents in Spain. The Germans sent out Focke-Wulf Condor aircraft to search for the convoy and three U-boats and four Italian submarines joined the hunt. A Condor sighted the convoy on 18 September but was driven off by a Fairey Fulmar plane. Next day it was spotted by an

Italian submarine and a German U-boat but the Italian vessel developed engine trouble and abandoned the pursuit.

On 20 September, two of the convoy's escorting destroyers left it but another destroyer took their place. The two Italian submarines then attacked the convoy but failed to damage it and on 22 September two more destroyers left the convoy and were replaced by another. Although the Italians continued to pursue the convoy they were unable to initiate an attack.

Two U-boats arrived on 25 September and began firing on the convoy. Several hits were scored and by midnight two vessels had been sunk. A corvette attacked one of the U-boats but without inflicting damage and a few hours later another U-boat sank two ships. When a coaster stopped to pick up survivors it was torpedoed and only 18 men survived out of the 109 men on the three sunken ships. They reached land after travelling on open seas in a lifeboat for two weeks.

In spite of these casualties one of the destroyers left the convoy on 26 September while four U-boats shadowed its progress. One U-boat was damaged by an Allied aircraft and was forced to retire but the others continued their pursuit.

On the night of 26 September, the three U-boats attacked and sank three ships. Next day they continued their pursuit and another vessel was sunk. After this they retired from the fray and returned to base and the rest of the convoy reached Liverpool safely on 1 October. Nine ships out of the original 25 that had set sail had been lost at sea, making it one of the worst disasters of the naval campaign.[25]

The southbound convoy OG-74 was attacked in the same region. Two U-boats stalked the convoy and sank five ships, though both submarines were damaged in the encounter and ran out of torpedoes and so were forced to return to base once more.[26]

CONVOY HG-76

The fierce battle between convoy HG-76 and German raiders was an important turning point in the Battle of the Atlantic. It was the first time the British had won a full-scale naval encounter and it gave great encouragement to the government.

The commander of the convoy, Commander 'Johnny' Walker, was an outspoken maverick who had been passed over for promotion numerous times because of his refusal to follow established rules. His time came with the war at sea reaching crisis point, when he was given command of convoy HG-76 sailing via Gibraltar to Britain. This gave him the opportunity to try out some of his radically different ideas about dealing with the U-boat menace.

There were 20 merchant ships in the convoy, accompanied by two Bittern-class sloops, seven corvettes, the aircraft carrier *Audacity*, three destroyers and eight Martlet planes. It was a strong escorting force but the Germans, having achieved success on this route already, were confident they could prevail.

On 8 November six Focke-Wulf Condor planes were sent in pursuit of convoy SL-91, bound from Sierra Leone to Liverpool. *Audacity*'s radar detected two of the Condors and sent a Martlet patrol to stop them from attacking. One of the Condors escaped but the other was shot down by the Martlet, though not before it had destroyed one of the British aircraft. Three hours later another Condor was shot down and a fourth escaped to safety. Both sides had lost a plane but the Germans had failed to direct U-boats towards the convoy.

On the other hand the Germans now knew that HG-76 was accompanied by an aircraft carrier and four U-boats set off in pursuit. They arrived on 17 December and a Martlet was launched from the carrier. It sank one of the submarines but the plane crashed and the pilot was killed.

A cat and mouse game between the convoy and its attackers followed, which turned into a ferocious naval encounter lasting five days. During the course of the battle four ships were sunk, including the aircraft carrier *Audacity*, while five U-boats were destroyed. The loss of so many submarines at once was unparalleled and caused consternation in the German navy. It was the first British victory in a naval battle against German submarines and represented a turning point in the war.[27]

December saw a slowdown in the eastern Atlantic conflict, when Allied ships failed to destroy many U-boats but most convoys reached their destinations safely. Shipping losses continued to be high but were not as disastrous as before.

AMERICA ENTERS THE WAR

Following the Japanese attack on Pearl Harbor and the declaration of war on the United States by Germany, Roosevelt had a free hand. The expectation of the majority of Americans was that he would prioritize the Pacific War against Japan and only play a peripheral role in the European conflict, particularly given the fact that Germany was in control of most of the landmasses of Europe. But Germany now had a new enemy to face and Dönitz began making plans to attack shipping off the east coast of the United States.

He was helped by the fact that America had not engaged in naval warfare on its own shores for nearly 100 years and had no idea of the kind of precautions to take. The authorities did not adopt the elementary expedient of a blackout, so blazing city lights at night offered easy sources of illumination to U-boats waiting off the shore. They were able to move in and attack with perfect visibility.

To make matters worse, when the Royal Navy recommended to the American fleet that they should introduce a blackout their

Anglophobe naval commander, Admiral Ernest King, rejected their advice. He was equally dismissive of suggestions that the United States should introduce a convoy system to protect its shipping. His apologists argue that the Americans lacked sufficient destroyers to protect convoys and so he believed they were better employed in protecting Allied troops than shepherding merchant shipping. These excuses had been used by the British during the early months of the war and were found to be false at that time. The Americans should have listened to the British, who had centuries of experience of naval war, but King preferred to go his own way.[28]

A more cogent objection to deploying American ships on convoy duty was the necessity to transport Lend-Lease supplies to the Soviet Union and keep the Pacific fleet ready for action against the Japanese. Even so, the failure to protect ships operating in home waters was – especially after the advice from the British, who had made a similar mistake about merchant shipping – a disastrous error. It led to what German U-boat crews referred to as the 'Second Happy Time', when their submarines inflicted significant casualties on American shipping without serious challenge.

OPERATION DRUMBEAT

In what was codenamed *Operation Paukenschlag* (Operation Drumbeat) German submarines entered US waters and began inflicting havoc. American troopships were safe but merchant shipping was devastated.[29]

Dönitz planned to attack shipping off the American East Coast, but he only had 12 Type IX boats that were able to reach US waters and six of them had been ordered by Hitler to serve in the Mediterranean. One of the others was under repair so Dönitz was only able to put five U-boats into the field to attack

American shipping, but he launched them with deadly effect.

In spite of the small numbers of U-boats available to Dönitz the effect on US shipping was out of all proportion. The Germans were assisted by mistakes made by the American navy which in spite of its inexperience in naval warfare still refused to take advice from the British. The result was unnecessary losses as the German submarines caused havoc.

On 13 January 1942 came the first U-boat incursions into American waters. The intruders remained there until 6 February and during that period they sank a total of 156,939 tons of shipping without the loss of a single submarine. Not until May did King introduce a convoy system and the result was the sinking of seven U-boats. Even with this belated security measure the naval war continued to go badly for the Americans. U-boats were able to close a number of US ports and they wrought havoc on shipping in the Caribbean and the Gulf of Mexico. Only when escort ships provided by the British began to arrive in July did the tide of war turn. The result was that the U-boats returned to the previous policy of attacking convoys in the North Atlantic.[30]

Operation Drumbeat convinced Hitler that Dönitz was correct about using U-boats primarily to raid commerce rather than attack warships, so he gave Dönitz a free hand to deploy and operate submarines according to his own ideas. Raeder was dismissed and Dönitz became the new head of the German navy.

THE FOCUS OF BATTLE SHIFTS

On 19 July 1942 Dönitz decided that the American conflict was no longer viable as the introduction of the convoy system by the US and the arrival of British escort ships to assist them led to a dramatic decline in the numbers of vessels sunk by U-boats. He then withdrew his fleet of submarines and by the end of

July redeployed them to the North Atlantic region. The result of his decision was a dramatic rise in shipping losses and October 1942 saw 56 ships totalling over 258,000 tons sunk in the gap between Greenland and Iceland. U-boat losses also rose. Twenty-one had been destroyed in the first six months of 1942 whereas in August and September 60 were sunk.[31]

Once again, the North Atlantic became a killing ground for merchant ships. German U-boats prowled with increasing success and the supply line to Britain was in danger of being reduced so drastically that real hardship loomed. In spite of rationing and attempts to produce as much food and other material as possible at home, the quantities were inadequate to overcome the losses being sustained.[32]

British naval resources were now unable to fulfil the demands made upon them. With merchant ships and vessels of war deployed in the North and South Atlantic, the Mediterranean, the Arctic and the Indian Ocean, the strain of fighting a global war was beyond British capabilities. Matters were made worse by the insistence of both America and Russia that an invasion of France needed to be undertaken in September 1942. Churchill was forced to go to Washington to speak directly with Roosevelt in June 1942 and spent two weeks arguing against the scheme. After the war he wrote:

> No responsible British military authority has so far been able to make a plan for September 1942 which has any chance of success unless the Germans become utterly demoralized, of which there is no likelihood.[33]

The fall of Tobruk and Rommel's continuing advance in North Africa changed Roosevelt's mind and he agreed to support the British campaign in North Africa. It is clear that Churchill was right to stand out against a premature invasion of France for which there were simply not enough ships or troops available. In addition, air superiority was not decisive enough. Roosevelt and Stalin were desperate to relieve the pressure on them but an assault on France in 1942 would have been a disastrous failure.

THE *LACONIA* TRAGEDY

On Saturday 12 September 1942 five U-boats were lurking in the South Atlantic, preparing to attack vessels in South African waters. That evening submarine *U-156* saw the liner *Laconia* heading northwards. The *Laconia* was sailing for Britain with nearly 3,000 people on board, including almost 2,000 Italian prisoners of war as well as Allied servicemen and 80 civilians. Its captain knew that U-boats were active in the area and tried to avoid the coast of Africa. Civilian liners were not legitimate targets under the rules of war, but the *Laconia* had been converted to an armed troopship on the outbreak of war, which meant that a U-boat was within its rights to attack it.

At 7 p.m. *U-156* fired two torpedoes at the ship and within 15 minutes the *Laconia* began sinking. The boilers of the ship then exploded, adding to the chaos. Those on board tried to get into lifeboats but others swam or floated on the water. When the U-boat captain observed the bodies in the water he attempted to help the survivors and after midnight he radioed Dönitz to ask for instructions on his course of action. Dönitz ordered him to rescue the survivors and instructed three U-boats in the area to join in the task. Even Hitler approved the rescue operation. Dönitz then ordered two further U-boats off the coast of West Africa to join their colleagues.

By early morning *U-156* was towing four lifeboats with 200 passengers aboard, including women and children. When the U-boat commander radioed for assistance, his message was received by the British authorities in Freetown, who immediately dismissed it as a trap. They did not pass on the call to naval vessels in the area, so they could assist in rescuing survivors. However, two Vichy French ships responded and began sailing towards the scene.

That evening an American pilot on his first mission flew overhead and sighted *U-156*. The captain ordered a large Red Cross flag to be displayed on the bridge of the submarine. It could not have been missed by the pilot. The U-boat captain then signalled the pilot in Morse code asking if there were any ships nearby, to which the pilot responded by demanding that the submarine should display its national flag. He then flew off and radioed his base for instructions. The order came back instantly: 'sink sub'.[34]

The American pilot dropped three bombs, all of which missed their target, and the U-boat responded by trying to cut the towlines to the lifeboats so it could submerge without drowning the survivors. Oblivious to what was happening, the pilot then dropped two further bombs, one of which exploded under the submarine's control room. The captain ordered all survivors on the deck of the U-boat to put on lifejackets and jump into the sea and then put his boat into a sharp dive. This confused the pilot, who reported to base that 'the sub rolled over and was last seen bottom up. Crew had abandoned sub and taken to surrounding lifeboats.'[35]

Everything about this statement is mistaken. The U-boat sustained only minor damage and had not been abandoned by its crew and the pilot should have been able to distinguish between an upturned lifeboat and a submarine that was 'bottom up'. He should also have queried why so many people were in the water in lifeboats, which were visible to him as his account makes clear, and he could have radioed base control again and asked for further clarification. Instead, he allowed his confused impressions to lead him to slaughter innocent people.

It is difficult to understand the orders of the base commander. The pilot was confused and inexperienced, but he was able to report to his superior officer that the U-boat was flying a Red Cross flag and that there were people in lifeboats. His base commander should then have hesitated before giving the command to sink a vessel in those circumstances. He could have contacted a higher authority or asked the British if they had received any messages from U-boats, but he did neither of those things and simply gave the order to destroy the submarine. Given the information he had received from the pilot, he must have known that his orders would lead to the deaths of innocent people as well as the crew of the U-boat. As it happened, none of the submariners were killed but over 1,000 innocent deaths resulted from his order.

The British decision to ignore the original message from the submarine and not send vessels to pick up survivors is indefensible. They should have investigated the possibility that the U-boat captain was asking them to collect survivors, as had been standard practice for the first three years of the war.

Dönitz was furious and ordered the captain of *U-156* to put the safety of his boat first and not concern himself with rescuing survivors. He heard that two other submarines had rescued almost 250 people, including women and children, and this led him to order the U-boats to wait and assist them until the Vichy ships arrived. In the meantime, he instructed them to place every survivor, except the Italian POWs, into lifeboats.

On 17 September the American pilot whose first flight had caused death and destruction to innocent people, but had inflicted neither casualties nor significant damage on the U-boat, returned to the scene. His bombs missed their target and accomplished nothing. By now even he must have known that civilians, Allied servicemen and POWs were on board but he continued his attack, which was mercifully ineffective.

Later that day French ships arrived and took most of the survivors on board. This was not the end of the story of the survivors of the *Laconia*. One of the lifeboats had been so thrown about by the waves that it became separated from the U-boats and drifted in the vast emptiness of the Atlantic Ocean. Out of the party of 68 on board the lifeboat only 16 survived, following an epic voyage of 25 days and 600 miles (960 km).

The *Laconia* set sail with a total of 2,730 passengers of whom 1,660 died. There is no doubt that but for the actions of the three U-boat captains the 1,000 who survived would have been lost. On the other hand, the gross, even criminal, negligence on the part of the British authorities and the recklessness of the American pilot and his base commander added needlessly to the death toll.

Furious at the way his crews had been put at risk while rescuing survivors, Dönitz issued what became known as the 'Laconia order'. On 17 September he issued this instruction to all U-boats:

> *All attempts to rescue the crew of sunken ships will cease forthwith. This prohibition applies equally to the picking up of men in the water and putting them aboard a lifeboat, to the righting of capsized lifeboats and to the supply of food and water. Such activities are a contradiction of the primary object of war, namely, the destruction of enemy ships and their crews.*[36]

Even the British and the Americans were embarrassed by their combination of negligence and incompetence and tried to conceal the scale of the disaster. The official position was that a 'mystery plane' was responsible for the catastrophe. It was 20 years before the truth was revealed.[37]

The anger felt by Dönitz and Hitler arose not simply out of the *Laconia* tragedy, but was the culmination of a series of violations of international maritime law involving British forces deliberately shooting survivors in the water, resulting in their death. Three incidents occurred during the Narvik campaign and nine during the battle for Crete in May 1941. On 4 July 1941 the British ship *Torbay* sank two German ships and used two Lewis guns on the bridge to kill the survivors and on 9 July the captain of the same ship refused to accept seven German prisoners. They were forced to board a large rubber float and were shot dead while in the water. Then on 12 May a British submarine attacked and sank a Greek vessel. The crew separated the Greeks from the Germans and allowed the Greeks to board a lifeboat before shooting the Germans. Given these examples of flagrant disregard for international maritime law and the Hague Convention, it is easier to understand Dönitz's fury. It is also possible to regard the 'Laconia Order' as a policy forced upon him by Allied violations rather than being just another example of Nazi brutality.[38]

The caveat is that such an order would have been given eventually as the tide of war altered. It remains difficult to defend the decision to prosecute Dönitz on the basis of the 'Laconia Order' when equally dubious behaviour was carried out by the Allies and never punished.

LOOMING DEFEAT

By August 1942 Dönitz achieved his target of 300 U-boats. The result was that the next five months saw a huge increase in sinkings, with 380 ships destroyed in the Atlantic for a total of 720,000 tons (653,000 tonnes).

Churchill was so alarmed at the carnage that he sent an anguished telegram to Roosevelt:

> *The U-boat menace is our worst danger. Not only does this attack cripple our war energies and threaten our life, but it arbitrarily limits the might of the United States coming into the struggle. The oceans, which were your shield, threaten to become your cage.*[39]

Churchill added that stocks of food in Britain were 'running down with dangerous rapidity' and if there was 'a renewed blitz on the Mersey and the Clyde' or a 'concentration of U-boats on the Atlantic routes' he would 'be forced to reduce our general commitment to the overseas war effort'.[40]

Roosevelt faced his own supply shortages with many advisers hostile to the idea of providing further support to Britain, so Churchill sent his Minister of Production, Oliver Lyttelton, to Washington to try and reach an agreement with the president. He faced serious opposition from senior American military and naval personnel, who threatened to 'cut off food exports' and reduce the level of supplies to Britain so the US could concentrate on the Pacific campaign. Lyttelton battled firmly against this opposition and presented his proposals to Roosevelt. The result was a typically ambiguous 'commitment' from the president, who promised that 'you may depend on the tonnage necessary to meet your import program' but added 'emergencies may develop which may require me to divert for our military purposes tonnage which it is now contemplated will be utilized for imports to Great Britain'.[41]

Events showed that Lyttelton's apparent success in obtaining this commitment was illusory. The War Shipping Administration (WSA) informed the British representative in Washington that 'any figures of tonnage are to be taken as estimates only, and not as commitment to allocate a precise amount of shipping'.[42]

Meanwhile, U-boats continued to sink shipping more rapidly than it could be replaced. Dönitz had 365 U-boats available and they accounted for 60 per cent of the 1,664 vessels destroyed. There was a million-ton deficit between ships built and ships sunk and supplies of food and oil were at critical levels.

The situation was so extreme and the obstructionism of the US made the British task so difficult that Churchill was compelled to send another appeal to Roosevelt. He told the president:

> *Unless our shipping resources are, in fact, as you so kindly propose I shall be forced immediately to reduce the British war effort in overseas theatres.*[43]

The naval war was at its height and Dönitz's U-boats were destroying such a volume of shipping that Britain was on the brink of defeat. At sea the situation for the country was as dangerous as it had been on land and in the air in 1940. Without an urgent increase in the production of ships on both sides of the Atlantic Britain was doomed.

NOTES

1 Padfield, *War Beneath the Sea*

2 Ernest Lindley, 'The Grand Alliance', *St. Joseph News-Press*, 30 Sept 1940. 'Until the outcome of the battle of the Atlantic can be more clearly foreseen, there would be high risks both to Japan and ourselves in becoming engaged in war.' H.J.J. Sargint, 'Mighty Nazi effort to invade England now in the making: Observers see amphibious attack as Hitler's anticipated thrust against British Isles', *Miami News*, 18 January 1941. 'This country is fighting a battle which may well be called the battle of the Atlantic, though it is not more than an extension of the battle of Britain.' Both of these uses of the term 'Battle of the Atlantic' predate Alexander's use.

3   *Dönitz*, op. cit.
4   William L. Langer, S. Gleason, S. Everett, *The Undeclared War 1940–1941: The World Crisis and American Foreign Policy*, Harper, 1953
5   Carlton Jackson, *Who Will Take Our Children? The British Evacuation Program of World War II*, McFarland, 2008
6   Bess Walder's account of her survival from the sinking of the *City of Benares*, Imperial War Museum archives
7   Dimbleby, op. cit.
8   Ibid.
9   Ibid.
10 Paul Lund and Harry Ludlam, *Night of the U-boats*, Foulsham, 1973
11 Ibid.
12 John Keegan, *The Price of Admiralty*, Viking, 1989
13 Padfield, *War Beneath the Waves*
14 Ibid.
15 Ibid.
16 Ibid.
17 '"Nazis Undoubtedly Sank the *Robin Moor*, Aware She Was a U.S. Ship", Consul Says', *New York Times*, 13 June 1941
18 Robert Dallek, *Franklin D. Roosevelt and American Foreign Policy, 1932–1945*, Oxford University Press, 1979
19 Squadron Leader James Thompson, account given to the Imperial War Museum
20 Account by merchant seaman John Bradbury, given by his daughter Kate Elliott to the BBC
21 Ibid.
22 Waldo Heinrichs, *Threshold of War: Franklin D. Roosevelt and American Entry into WWII*, Oxford University Press, 1988
23 Franklin D. Roosevelt, 'Fireside Chat', 11 September 1941, in: www.presidency. ucsb.edu/>pid=16012/
24 Ibid.
25 Clay Blair, *Hitler's U-boat War: The Hunters 1939–1942*, Random House, 1996
26 Arnold Hague, *The Allied Convoy System*, Vanwell, 2000
27 Terence Robertson, *Walker RN: Britain's Ace U-Boat Killer*, Pan, 1958
28 Samuel Eliot Morison, *The Battle of the Atlantic: 1939–1945*, Little, Brown, 1947
29 Michael Gannon, *Operation Drumbeat*, Naval Institute Press, 1990
30 Philip Kaplan, *Grey Wolves: The U-boat War 1939–1945*, Pen & Sword, 2014
31 John Costello and Terry Hughes, *The Battle of the Atlantic*, Collins, 1977
32 Ibid.
33 Winston S. Churchill, *The Second World War, vol. IV, The Hinge of Fate*, Cassell, 1953
34 S.W. Roskill, *The War at Sea, 1939–1945, vol. II – The Period of Balance*, Naval and Military Press, 2004

35 Ibid.
36 *Dönitz*, op. cit.
37 Maurer Maurer and Lawrence J. Paszek, 'Origin of the Laconia Order,' *Journal of the Royal United Service Institute for Defence Studies* vol. 109, no. 636, November 1964
38 F. Grossmith, *The Sinking of the Laconia, A Tragedy in the Battle of the Atlantic*, Watkins Publishing, 1994
39 Churchill's telegram to Roosevelt, 31 October 1942, given in: Francis L. Loewenheim, Harold D. Langley and Manfred Jones (eds) *Roosevelt and Churchill: Their Secret Correspondence*, Barrie and Jenkins, 1995
40 Ibid.
41 Ibid.
42 Kevin Smith, *Conflict Over Convoys: Anglo-American Logistics Diplomacy in the Second World War*, Cambridge University Press, 2002
43 Roskill, op. cit.

CHAPTER FIVE

THE BATTLE OF THE ATLANTIC – SECOND PHASE

On 3 January 1943 a U-boat near Trinidad observed a convoy of oil tankers heading north. The captain contacted Berlin and Dönitz ordered a wolfpack to attack. There were eight U-boats in the group and by 8 January they had detected convoy TM-1. The nine tankers were escorted by three corvettes and a destroyer but the submarines still attacked when they came within range.

CATASTROPHE IN THE SOUTH ATLANTIC

For three days the wolfpack engaged in a killing spree. The four escorts were unable to protect the merchant ships and seven of the nine tankers were destroyed with considerable loss of life, only two reaching Gibraltar. It did not help matters when the radar sets in two of the corvettes failed, which compounded the poor quality of defence provided by the escorts. The loss of such a crucial material as oil was hugely significant and the death toll of merchant seamen rose inexorably. If the current rate of attrition continued, the Germans would win the Battle of the Atlantic in a few months.[1]

DISASTER LOOMING

January was a bad month for the Allies with 38 merchant ships sunk and February was even worse. Sixty-three ships were destroyed in that month. March saw a major naval battle between three wolfpacks and two Allied convoys when convoys SC-122 and HX-229, totalling 110 ships between them and with 13 warships as escorts, were waylaid by U-boats. A desperate battle followed between 40 submarines and the convoys, which lasted three days.

Twenty-one ships totalling 141,000 tons were sunk, more than 300 merchant seamen died and just one U-boat was lost. It was the deadliest single U-boat attack of the war and the culmination of 20 days of raiding that saw half a million tons of Allied shipping lost. The month of March saw 97 Allied ships destroyed.[2]

The effect of the disastrous toll on shipping forced a radical change in British strategy. Until this time the RAF had concentrated most of its resources on bombing Germany and when Admiral Sir Max Horton demanded greater air cover for the Battle of the Atlantic an immediate conflict arose between the Navy and the RAF. When Horton was appointed commander of the Western Approaches in November 1942, he attempted to push forward his new approach to naval warfare, which emphasized the importance of technology and training and demanded 'a reasonable number of long-endurance destroyers and long-range aircraft'.[3] He was given the destroyers he required and the crews to man them were trained, but the RAF continued to resist his request for air cover. In January 1943 Horton pressed his case to Sir Stafford Cripps, Minister of Aircraft Production. Cripps agreed with Horton's assessment and put his proposals to the War Cabinet.

In spite of Cripps' support, the RAF opposed diverting aircraft from bombing raids to convoy protection. Only the shock of the catastrophic toll on merchant shipping during March persuaded Air Marshal Sir Charles Portal to provide 150 Liberator planes to Coastal Command.

This decision caused a split in the Cabinet with Lord Cherwell, Churchill's scientific adviser, declaring: 'It is difficult to compare the damage done to any of the forty odd big German cities in a 1,000 ton raid with the advantage of sinking one U-boat out of 400 and saving 3 or 4 ships out of 5,500.'[4]

Air Chief Marshal Sir Arthur 'Bomber' Harris was enraged and declared that an intensive bombing campaign could 'knock Germany out of the war'.[5] With both Harris and Cherwell denouncing Horton's plans, Churchill had to decide between the conflicting priorities.

Temperamentally, Churchill's sympathies were with the bombing campaign. On the other hand, the Navy had always been close to his heart and he recognized the crucial importance of keeping Britain's supply lines open. The carnage inflicted on shipping during March persuaded him to grant Horton's request and provide Coastal Command with the aircraft it needed. Cherwell and Harris raged against his decision but Churchill was adamant. His decision was not only correct but fundamentally changed the balance of the naval war in favour of the Allies.

THE TIDE TURNS

March 1943 was a disastrous month for the Allies but it provided their first glimmer of hope. Coastal Command's enhanced air cover allowed them to launch devastating bombing raids against U-boats as they left the Bay of Biscay to prepare for their attacks.

In the first week of March, *U-333* encountered the first use of the Allies' improved radar system, which operated on a 10 cm (4 in) wavelength and had a range of up to 60 miles (96 km). The submarine suddenly found itself caught in the bright beams of an aircraft searchlight and the crew saw a flare that had 'just jumped out of the darkness' preparing to attack them.[6]

Reacting quickly, the U-boat captain ordered his crew to train their guns on the aircraft. They landed a direct hit and the Vickers Wellington burst into flames. Before it sank to the ocean it dropped four bombs. Two missed their target, one failed to explode and the fourth caused only superficial damage.

What disturbed the submarine captain most was that Metox 600, the previously infallible radar detector that was fitted to all U-boats, had failed to pick up the aircraft. The news was passed on to Berlin and Dönitz immediately realized that the Allies were using a new radar frequency that Metox 600 was unable to detect.[7] This unexpected development made Dönitz uneasy for the first time. The combination of the new radar system and the increase in air cover meant that his U-boats were more exposed than previously and their chances of detecting the enemy were dramatically reduced. He began by ordering all U-boat captains in range of Allied aircraft to remain beneath the surface at night and only come up in the daytime for battery charging. This tactic made no difference, so Dönitz equipped submarines with anti-aircraft guns, ordering the boats 'to stay on the surface and fight it out'.[8]

This strategy disconcerted the Allies at first but it was as futile as the Kamikaze attacks by Japanese pilots. The Atlantic had been the only theatre of war in which the Germans were winning and now they were being defeated on that front as well. Although the war dragged on for two more years, German dominance was at an end. It was no longer a question of if but when the Allies achieved final victory.

DÖNITZ FIGHTS BACK

The first attempt to counter the superiority of the Allies in the naval war was a direct request by Dönitz to Hitler. He asked for the building of 800 new U-boats and for 40,000 sailors to be recruited to man them. Hitler, by now convinced that German submarines could win the naval war, agreed to his demands.

His other request was for bombers and MRCAs (multirole combat aircraft) to protect the U-boat bases in France, but Göring opposed this idea and Hitler was only able to effect a compromise solution. Dönitz was promised Ju-88 fighters to assist him in the Bay of Biscay, but Hitler did not make the MRCAs available to him as he had requested. Later, Dönitz was to describe the lack of air support as 'one of the gravest handicaps under which we suffered'.[9]

As was the case throughout the war, the B-Dienst, the German navy's signal intelligence agency, continued to crack the British naval code. This allowed the Germans to plot the course of convoys in advance and minimize danger to the attacking U-boats.

Dönitz ordered his crews to redouble their efforts and make one final push to try and win the Battle of the Atlantic. They responded bravely but courage alone was not sufficient. A combination of factors came together that made a German victory impossible.

BLACK MAY

May 1943 saw the final defeat of the U-boats. They continued to fight until the end but from that time onwards it was a losing battle. Radar, lack of air cover and a sharp increase in the number of ships available to the Allies doomed them.

This increased shipping capacity came about for two main reasons. One was that victory in the Mediterranean naval war freed up British vessels for service in the Atlantic. This, together with de Gaulle's Free French forces now controlling French colonies in Africa and adding the French navy's resources to the Allied fleet, made a huge difference to the number of ships available for deployment. The other reason was the 'Liberty' ships. The first Liberty ship, the *Patrick Henry*, was launched on 27 September 1941 by President Roosevelt. It was the first of a series of 9,000-ton freighters. The Liberty ships were the brainchild of Henry Kaiser, the son of a German immigrant, who had previous experience of building ships in sections that were welded together rather than riveted.

With the outbreak of war demand for these Liberty ships accelerated. The design was basic with 'no electricity or running water for the crew' and the ships had 'no fire detection system'.[10] At the beginning each ship took 200 days to complete but that figure dropped dramatically. The record time for building one of the Liberty ships was five days, but by early 1943 the average construction time was 45 days. This enabled large numbers of the ungainly freighters to be produced quickly and they swamped the German attack capability to the point where there was a constant surplus of new shipping over vessels sunk. This imbalance made it impossible for the Germans to win the naval war.[11]

To make matters worse for Dönitz, May saw a series of battles between U-boats and convoys. The first was convoy ONS-5 which set sail from Liverpool on 21 April 1943. Its destination was Halifax in Canada and it consisted of 40 freighters with an escort of seven warships. When the convoy's messages were detected by B-Dienst, Dönitz despatched 39 U-boats to attack the target.

Nine Liberty cargo ships docked at the outfitting yard of the California Shipbuilding Corporation, Los Angeles are readied for delivery to the US Maritime Commission, December 1943.

On the afternoon of 4 May the wolfpack began its attack. During the next few hours, five freighters were sunk. Most of the ships' crews also perished. Next evening the U-boats returned and sank a further seven ships for the loss of one submarine. The convoy appeared doomed but the weather came to its rescue. On the morning of 6 May, a thick fog sprang up which made the ships almost invisible to the submarines. By contrast the ships' radar could identify the U-boats quickly. The convoy began to attack the wolfpack and six U-boats were sunk. Twelve ships had also been lost, but a ratio of one submarine for two freighters represented a defeat and Dönitz admitted that such a rate of attrition was unsustainable.[12]

The now routine air cover for convoys deterred many submarines from attacking at all. Those that continued to strike against shipping failed disastrously and by the end of the month a total of 41 U-boats had been destroyed.[13]

THE CASABLANCA CONFERENCE

The Casablanca Conference took place from 14 to 24 January 1943 and its purpose was to plan the Allies' European strategy for the remainder of the war. Winston Churchill and Franklin D. Roosevelt were the two main players as Joseph Stalin did not attend. The conference decided that the U-boat menace was the greatest threat to the Allies and from then onwards most of Britain's war efforts were focused on defeating it. Within five months Britain had beaten Dönitz's wolfpacks and the road to victory in the Atlantic was clear at last.

This change in the naval campaign was seized on by Roosevelt and Churchill as a way of placating Stalin. They promised to 'launch large-scale amphibious operations at the earliest moment' against the Italians. In addition, they declared that a cross-Channel invasion of France would be undertaken 'as soon as practicable' and that in the meantime they would carry out an intensive bombing campaign against Germany 'at a rapid rate'.[14]

THE TRIDENT CONFERENCE
May 1943 saw a visit by Churchill to Washington to meet with Roosevelt. This meeting, called the Trident Conference, lasted for 14 days and as at Casablanca military advisers from both Britain and America were present. Once more conflicting priorities led to angry exchanges. Brooke wrote scathingly in his diary:

> *King will remain determined to press Pacific at the expense of all other fronts. Marshall wishes to ensure cross-Channel operation at expense of Mediterranean.*[15]

Churchill managed to persuade Roosevelt to focus on defeating Germany before Japan, but a series of arguments followed about whether the attack on Sicily should be followed by an invasion of Italy or whether France should be the next objective. It was finally agreed that the invasion of France would be launched in spring 1944.

On the Atlantic front, King requested General Henry Arnold to send a squadron of B-24s to Newfoundland to strengthen the air cover for convoys. However, Arnold decided to instruct his pilots to engage in purely offensive missions against U-boats or German ships and not to carry out escort duties for convoys. This created another bone of contention between the British and the Americans, as the overstretched British and Canadian forces were being asked to carry out operations without sufficient numbers.

THE SOUTH ATLANTIC FRONT
The South Atlantic was never as active a theatre of the naval war as the North Atlantic but it saw considerable activity,

principally by U-boats. German attacks began as early as the autumn of 1940 but it was not until 1941 that these caused serious concern to the Americans. Following negotiations with Brazil, the United States sent military assistance to the country and from April 1942 German and Italian submarines began operating in Brazilian waters.[16] A series of attacks on merchant vessels led to Brazil declaring war on Germany and Italy on 22 August 1942 and this addition of naval strength helped the Allies in the South Atlantic, which was an area where Axis forces had operated with relative impunity.

The Brazilian navy was small, but its minelayers helped protect convoys and its planes gave air cover to ships in the area. It operated mainly in the Caribbean and South Atlantic areas and escorted over 3,000 ships with relative success. Only three of its warships were sunk but 32 of its merchant ships were attacked by U-boats, with a total loss of just over 1,000 people.

In July 1943, the Brazilian and American air forces co-ordinated their activities and succeeded in sinking *U-199*. Ten other German submarines were sunk by the Brazilians between January and September 1943 and by the autumn of 1943 the German threat to shipping had been virtually eliminated. A small band of submarines continued to operate until as late as March 1945 but most were withdrawn by summer 1944.

DEADLY JUNE

Black May was the turning point in the Battle of the Atlantic but the Germans fought on, employing the new tactic of attacking only by daylight. On 10 June five U-boats formed a pack off the French coast. They headed towards Cape Finisterre, with air cover from three Ju-88s until darkness fell.

Next morning the RAF arrived in the form of four bombers preparing to attack. The submarines remained on the surface and began firing at the planes, which deterred them from attacking, and after two hours the aircraft retreated.

Two days later a Sunderland flying boat discovered the pack. It began to attack the U-boats but they returned fire. The plane was damaged but the guns jammed on two of the boats and the Sunderland crew seized the chance to drop seven bombs, four of them hitting one of the U-boats. However, another submarine managed to hit the plane, which crashed into the water, killing its three-man crew. The submarine crew searched the bodies of the dead men and found what the captain considered to be important documents, which he decided to forward to Germany. As the damaged U-boat was incapable of further attacks, the pack leader decided to shepherd it back to base while the other three boats continued their journey.

On the morning of 14 June two bombers appeared. The escorting U-boat fired and hit one of the aircraft, which ironically was a Focke-Wolf Fw 200 Condor, and both planes retreated. At 1 p.m. an RAF bomber emerged and circled the two submarines. The guns of the escort boat jammed and the other boat could not fire for fear of hitting the other submarine, so the two boats were defenceless. The plane then dropped two depth charges and sank the already stricken U-boat while the other submarine dived beneath the surface, where it remained submerged for over an hour. The captain surfaced to find the plane gone and so he was able to rescue 19 survivors.

Later eight Ju-88s arrived to provide aerial cover and an hour and a half afterwards two destroyers appeared and collected the survivors of the sunken U-boat. They also took away the documents from the downed plane.

In terms of numbers this incident was not dramatic, with just two planes and one U-boat destroyed, but it made it clear to Dönitz that attempting to sail out of the Bay of Biscay on the surface was no longer an option as Allied air superiority was too great. He therefore reluctantly ordered his U-boats to 'proceed through Biscay mainly submerged'.[17]

The importance of the Bay of Biscay as a base from which U-boats could sail out into the Atlantic was clear to the Allies, who took measures to make it impossible for submarines to use it effectively. U-boats that emerged at night to recharge their batteries had previously been able to do so in relative safety, but following the invention of the Leigh Light this became much more dangerous.

The Leigh Light was a searchlight mounted under a plane which was switched on as soon as the submarine moved out of radar detection range. This enabled the aircraft to identify and attack the U-boat before it had a chance to dive successfully.[18] The German response was to provide air cover to U-boats leaving or returning to the area, which helped to protect the boats slightly. However, its effect was greatly minimized by information passed on by resistance workers in the ports.

GERMAN COUNTERMEASURES

The effect of the sudden increase in Allied numbers, the growing provision of air cover for convoys and the new radar system which made U-boats easily detectable combined to create an environment that made them much less effective. In retaliation, the Germans attempted to equip U-boats with more sophisticated torpedoes and anti-aircraft defences. The T-5 torpedo was superior to its predecessors and Dönitz hoped it could transform the situation. New methods of detecting radar were also developed and when *Schnorchels* (snorkels) were fitted to new U-boats it meant that they could run their diesel engines while submerged.

Armed with these new devices, the Germans returned to battle in the Atlantic in September 1943. Twenty-one U-boats were based to the south of Greenland with orders to intercept convoys travelling west as they entered an area where air cover was poor.

They launched successful attacks on convoys ONS-18 and ON-202. ONS-18 left Liverpool on 12 September 1943 bound for Halifax. It comprised 27 ships with an escort of five corvettes, a frigate, two destroyers and an aircraft carrier. When the wolfpack moved towards the convoy, it was reinforced by closing up to the convoy following it, ON-202. A support group was also sent to join the convoys.

ON-202 comprised a convoy of 38 ships that had left Liverpool on 15 September. It was escorted by three corvettes, two destroyers and a frigate. Between them the 65 merchant ships were now escorted by 19 warships. However, they still came under attack from 21 U-boats. U-270 fired a T-5 torpedo and damaged a ship before escaping after the escorts launched a counter-attack and two of the vessels were forced to abandon the convoy and return to base for repairs.

Air patrols then attacked the wolfpack and one U-boat was sunk and another damaged. On the night of 20–21 September the pack returned and two ships were sunk. Next day eight submarines launched an attack and sank two ships with one U-boat damaged. On the following night the attacks resumed, but this time one U-boat was sunk and three more were damaged. Hits were reported by the submarine crews but these claims turned out to be incorrect.

On 23 September fog in the Grand Banks area gave the opportunity to U-238 to penetrate the escorts and sink three ships. *U-666* sank a further vessel and *U-952* sank one ship and damaged another. The U-boat crews claimed to have sunk 21 ships and damaged two more but the reality was that nine ships were lost and another was damaged. On the German side, three U-boats were damaged and three destroyed.

The bulk of the ships arrived safely and though the new torpedo had been a success and had surprised the Allies the shipping loss rate was tolerable. Although the Germans had enjoyed initial success in the conflict it rapidly ended, with fewer ships sunk and more submarines lost. This had been the Kriegsmarine's first major foray into the North Atlantic since Black May but the boats now had to be withdrawn. Eight merchant ships and six warships had been sunk at a cost of 39 U-boats and such a casualty ratio made continuing the campaign impossible. All the U-boats could realistically do was launch surprise attacks in British waters and in 1944 many were commandeered to resist the coming invasion of France.

The loss of German bases in North Africa and Italy was crucial in terms of the Allies being able to supply their ships and troops and by the time D-Day arrived the Germans had lost the Battle of the Atlantic. The result was carnage for the U-boats and the loss of French bases as the Allies liberated France.

THE FINAL CONFLICT

The Germans had high hopes for their new Elektroboot. There were two variants of this design, the Type XXI and the short-range Type XXIII. The designs for the Type XXI were laid down in January 1943 and production began in 1944. It could run at 17 knots (19.5 mph) underwater and might have made a useful contribution to the war effort. However, it took around 18 months to build. By 1945 only five of the smaller Type XXIII U-boats were in service and one Type XXI. The Type XXIII carried out nine patrols and sank five ships while the Type XXI made one patrol and did not succeed in making contact with the enemy.

As the tide of the war turned relentlessly against the Germans, submarine bases in north Germany became more vulnerable. Over 200 U-boats were scuttled, though some tried to escape to Norwegian bases. Twenty-three U-boats were sunk in the Baltic during the first week of May while attempting to escape to Norway.

America saw the last U-boat action on 5–6 May 1945, when two U-boats were sunk and one ship destroyed, and on 7–8 May, a few hours before the final surrender of the German government, the final engagements of the Battle of the Atlantic took place. An RAF Catalina sank a U-boat and a submarine torpedoed three ships. And then the Battle of the Atlantic, like the war in Europe, was over at last. For the first four years of the naval conflict, it had been a close-run series of encounters and German victory was entirely possible, but the men who served by air and sea narrowly saved the Allies from defeat.

NOTES

1   Richard Woodman, *The Real Cruel Sea: The Merchant Navy in the Battle of the Atlantic, 1939–1943*, Pen and Sword, 2011
2   Hague, op. cit.
3   Rear Admiral W.S. Chalmers, *Max Horton and the Western Approaches*, Hodder and Stoughton, 1954
4   S.W. Roskill, *Churchill and the Admirals*, Pen and Sword, 2004
5   Dimbleby, op. cit.
6   Peter Cremer, *U-333: The Story of a U-boat Ace*, Triad Grafton, 1986
7   *Dönitz*, op. cit.
8   Ibid.
9   Ibid.
10 Arthur Herman, *Freedom's Forge: How American Business Produced Victory in World War II*, Random House, 2012

11 Albert P. Heiner, *Henry J. Kaiser: Western Colossus*, Halo, 1991
12 Dimbleby, op. cit.
13 Ibid.
14 Anne Armstrong, *Unconditional Surrender: The impact of the Casablanca policy upon World War II*, Rutgers University Press, 1961
15 Field Marshal Lord Alanbrooke, *War Diaries, 1939–1945*, Phoenix Press, 2002
16 C. Carey, *Galloping Ghosts of the Brazilian Coast*, iUniverse, 2004
17 Robert C. Stern, *Battle Beneath the Waves: The U-boat War*, Arms and Armour, 1999
18 Martin Bowman, *Deep Sea Hunters: RAF Coastal Command and the War Against the U-Boats and the German Navy 1939–1945*, Pen and Sword, 2014

CHAPTER SIX

THE BATTLE OF THE MEDITERRANEAN

Until Italy entered the war in 1940 the Mediterranean theatre was quiet. Germany was not initially involved in the region and at first the naval war was exclusively between the Italians and the British.

The fall of France removed the threat from the French navy and on paper the Italian position was strong. Mussolini possessed the largest surface fleet in the Mediterranean and the largest concentration of submarines. Added to that, the new Vichy government in France had not only made peace with Germany but was considered sympathetic to the Nazis, particularly by the British. With such a large navy in the Mediterranean the strength of the French fleet, if added to the Italian navy, would make Britain's position in the area untenable.

THE BRITISH HOLD OFF

The British were reluctant to turn on an ally and began negotiating with some of the French regional commanders. In Egypt this went well and French and British commanders agreed to place the French squadron at Alexandria beyond German reach. However, the situation with the main French fleet at Mers-el-Kebir in Algeria was different and they flatly refused to co-operate. The result was that British Force H from Gibraltar – a

British naval formation which comprised two aircraft carriers, a battleship, seven destroyers and a cruiser – bombarded the fleet and destroyed the bulk of it, which led the Vichy government to break off diplomatic relations with Britain and send aircraft to attack Gibraltar. In spite of this brief explosion of anger, only two naval encounters took place between Vichy and British forces during the remainder of the war.

The size of the Italian navy was not matched by its efficiency and Hitler soon discovered that Mussolini was more of a liability than an asset. Following a series of disastrous military and naval reverses in 1941 the Germans were compelled to rescue their ally. The Italian defeats in North Africa and Greece gave the Allies an opportunity to strike back and Hitler knew he had to intervene to prevent disaster. Among other things, this involved sending German U-boats into the Mediterranean. Dönitz protested the order but still obeyed it.

The first direct involvement of U-boats in the Mediterranean came in 1941, but on the outbreak of war on 3 September 1939 the Germans decided to attack ships in the Gibraltar area through the use of submarines. However, their dismal failure led them to abandon the idea.

On 2 October the first convoy bound for Gibraltar set sail from Land's End in Cornwall. There were 37 ships in convoy OG-1 and Dönitz decided to send three U-boats to attack them. The pack met up to the south-west of Ireland before moving off to Gibraltar.

But Dönitz's plan failed completely, with one U-boat unable to make any contact and being redirected to attack a French convoy near Cape Ortegal. The captain of the U-boat then fired four torpedoes at one of the ships but none exploded, so the frustrated submariner surfaced and sank the ship with gunfire.

An aerial view of British cruisers and aircraft carriers escorting convoys,
which are carrying supplies and reinforcements to Malta, August 1942.

His U-boat was damaged in the process and he was forced to return home.

The second U-boat, having waited fruitlessly off the coast of Ireland to rendezvous with the first boat, was directed to head towards Gibraltar and link up with the other two submarines. Instead of continuing to Gibraltar, the U-boat's commander decided to attack a convoy and began stalking it, but was forced to retreat owing to a shortage of fuel.

Only one U-boat remained available to attack shipping. It finally reached Gibraltar and attempted to lay mines across the harbour but a combination of anti-submarine patrols, bad weather and searchlights forced its captain to abandon the project, so he reloaded his boat with torpedoes and sailed into the Mediterranean. The BdU War Diary reported the operation as follows:

> *U-26 entered port. She did not carry out her minelaying operation off Gibraltar as the weather there was too bad. She was afterwards in the Mediterranean, as ordered, but apparently struck a poor time for traffic.*[1]

This fiasco led Dönitz to abandon any thoughts of sending U-boats into the Mediterranean and he never attempted to do so until Hitler ordered him to engage there in 1941. The collapse of France and the entry of Italy into the war caused panic in the Royal Navy, to the extent that a proposal to evacuate armed forces from the Mediterranean entirely was considered by the War Cabinet and strongly supported by Admiral Pound. Britain was overstretched and advocates of the plan argued that it enabled naval resources to be concentrated on the vital Atlantic supply route.

However, Churchill rejected the idea out of hand, declaring that it would be seen as a sign of surrender. It might also strain the loyalty of Australia, New Zealand and South Africa and encourage a swathe of anti-British movements in Iraq, Iran, Egypt and India. Control of the Suez Canal was vital and the only realistic option was to take the war to Italy.

The British attacked the Italian fleet with considerable success. For all its superiority in numbers in the Mediterranean, the Italian navy was no match for the Royal Navy. Its surface ships were bombed by the RAF and outfought at sea. Italy had the second largest submarine fleet in the world but its boats were slow, could not submerge quickly and found it difficult to evade enemy aircraft. It quickly became clear they were unsuited to combat in the Mediterranean and in spite of individual successes the Italian navy was badly beaten by the British.

Matters came to a head after the Italian invasion of Greece, when the Greeks repelled the invaders and prepared to liberate Albania from Italian occupation. A furious Hitler was compelled to save his ally from the consequences of his megalomania.

U-BOATS TO THE RESCUE

There was a huge difference in tactics between Dönitz's U-boat fleet and Italy's submarines. The Italians had a defensive mindset, preferring their enemies to approach their boats before releasing their torpedoes while still submerged. On the other hand, German submarine crews were trained to surface and attack their targets.

Initially the Italians were successful but the botched invasion of Greece altered the situation. On 8 December an Italian convoy of ten merchant ships, escorted by six destroyers and with four more destroyers and two cruisers providing defence, was waylaid by two British destroyers and two cruisers. The convoy was destroyed and essential supplies for Italian troops in Albania were lost.

On 11 November worse was to come as a number of Fairey Swordfish planes were launched from the aircraft carrier *Illustrious*. The aircraft ravaged the Italian fleet at Taranto and destroyed three battleships, two cruisers and two auxiliary vessels. On 15 December this disaster and a series of other setbacks forced the head of the Italian navy to resign.[2] By spring 1941 the Italians were struggling by land and sea. Raeder and Dönitz believed Germany's naval resources were too slender to enable them to assist their allies but Hitler rejected their advice. On 17 September he ordered six U-boats to enter the Mediterranean and base themselves at Salamis. Their mission was to disrupt British ships supplying Egypt and the eastern Mediterranean.

By 5 October all six U-boats had successfully entered the Mediterranean, slipping past the British ships stationed at Gibraltar, but the initial results were not encouraging. By the end of October two ships had been sunk and one was damaged, while one U-boat was forced to dock in Salamis for repairs. Dönitz was not impressed with this meagre haul and repeated his objections to using his U-boats in the Mediterranean rather than the Atlantic, but he was again overruled by Hitler.[3]

THE SINKING OF THE *ARK ROYAL*

The first major success for the Germans in the Battle of the Mediterranean occurred on 16 November 1941, after Italian aircraft reported the sailing of Gibraltar's Force H. The fleet was returning to Gibraltar after a successful attack on an Italian convoy and the delivery of 14 aircraft to Malta to assist in the defence of the island.

U-81 decided to attack the fleet and stalked it on its route to Gibraltar. At 4.36 p.m. torpedoes were fired at the vessels and the destroyers responded with depth charges. For five hours the submarine took evasive action before resurfacing.

The U-boat captain knew he had hit one of the ships but had no idea which one or how much damage he had inflicted. He then withdrew his boat and returned to base.

The *Ark Royal* was one of the prize aircraft carriers of the Royal Navy. When the torpedo struck the ship was rocked by the impact and the vessel filled with smoke. The captain initially thought there might have been an internal explosion, but as the carrier began listing towards starboard the captain realized that his ship had been hit by a torpedo. Lights began to go out on the ship and the electrical systems started to fail. At the same time, water was entering the vessel and widening the breach made by the torpedo.

The captain transferred almost 1,500 crew members to the destroyer *Legion*, which took half an hour. During this process the flooding of the ship increased. In a desperate attempt to save the carrier, the tugboat *Thames* tried to tow the *Ark Royal* back to Gibraltar, but in spite of the tug's best efforts the carrier continued to sink and fires broke out on the ship. Eventually there was no prospect of saving the vessel and the captain gave the order to abandon ship. By the evening of the following day the proud *Ark Royal* sank beneath the waves. Incredibly, only one crew member died.

When the Germans realized it was the *Ark Royal* that had been sunk by *U-81* they were delighted and the boat's commander was awarded a Knight's Cross.[4]

DISASTER IN THE EASTERN MEDITERRANEAN
Following the sinking of the *Ark Royal*, there were angry exchanges between Churchill and Admiral Sir Andrew

Here we see the British aircraft carrier Ark Royal's last moments from a Catalina flying boat, before it plunges to the bottom of the Med. It was the victim of a U-boat torpedo. The photograph shows a view of the side of the damaged ship as the carrier tips before sinking for ever.

Cunningham, commander of the Mediterranean fleet. On 24 November Cunningham took personal charge of a battle fleet attempting to intercept two Italian convoys bound for Benghazi with supplies.

Dönitz ordered his U-boats to concentrate their efforts on the route between Alexandria and Tobruk. He then instructed five submarines to relocate from the western Mediterranean to their new area of operations. On 25 November *U-331*, one of Dönitz's relocated boats, spotted Cunningham's battle fleet. The submarine's captain submerged and waited until three battleships and four destroyers came into view.

U-331 fired four torpedoes and promptly submerged. The battleship HMS *Barham* was hit and the U-boat escaped before the ships could reach it. Following the attack, the *Barham* sank rapidly and nearly 900 men were killed.[5]

Worse followed on 18 December, when an Italian submarine drew near to Alexandria and secured time bombs under two battleships and a destroyer. All three devices exploded and incapacitated the ships. Combined with the loss of the *Barham* to *U-331*, this was a catastrophe for the Royal Navy. Churchill wrote later:

> *In the course of a few weeks the whole of our Eastern Mediterranean battle fleet was eliminated as a fighting force.*[6]

Matters were no better in the western Mediterranean. Royal Navy losses included a yacht and an anti-submarine trawler, both sunk in a single attack by *U-374*. On 14 December a cruiser was sunk by *U-557* off the coast of Alexandria and in the same month three cruisers and a destroyer were sunk by German mines.

Only 12 merchant ships had been lost by the end of December but British naval strength in the Mediterranean had been decimated. The navy in Alexandria was reduced to three cruisers and a handful of destroyers while the position in Gibraltar was even worse. Only one aircraft carrier, one battleship and a cruiser remained, with just five U-boats being lost during the carnage.

U-BOAT BASES RELOCATE

It was decided that Salamis harbour did not have the capacity to deal with the increased volume of U-boats operating in the Mediterranean. Naples and Brindisi were considered as possible alternative bases, but La Spezia was finally settled on as the most suitable location, though German U-boats had to share their facilities with the Italian navy.

The base was strongly defended, with four coastal guns, four anti-aircraft guns and (from 1943) six 88 mm batteries. In addition, the Sarzana air base provided fighter cover for the submarine fleet and until the Italian surrender in 1943 it was strongly defended. The Allies bombed La Spezia heavily and damaged the town and the harbour but as the majority of civilians had been evacuated casualties were small. Most of the U-boats in the Mediterranean were based at La Spezia, with the rest being divided between Salamis, Pola and other bases. However, unlike some other German bases, there were no bunkers for the U-boats.[7]

BRITISH SUBMARINES IN THE MEDITERRANEAN

From the beginning of the war British submarines had been mishandled. They failed completely in the Norwegian campaign and were ineffective as escorts for convoys in the Atlantic.

Their failure in the North Sea and the Atlantic was disappointing, but it did not have serious consequences. In the Mediterranean, though, their misuse nearly led to disaster. By the end of 1940 the Italians had successfully transported large quantities of oil, along with troops and supplies, to Greece and North Africa without serious opposition. Only nine Italian ships and one submarine were sunk for the loss of nine British submarines.

New boats were sent to the Mediterranean to replace the lost submarines. These were based at Malta, which was an ideal position from which to attack Italian supply lines. The new submarines made little difference, however, and by March 1941 half a million tons of Axis supplies had reached North Africa, with only six ships sunk. Only 20,000 tons of supplies to Libya were lost.[8]

There were not enough boats at Malta to attack the Italian fleet successfully. Also, the Italians had changed their naval code on entering the war and Bletchley Park had not succeeded in cracking the new cipher.[9] Compounding inadequate resources and lack of intelligence about the disposition of convoys was the poor quality of British submarines. The British boats were slow, they carried only two torpedoes and their equipment was completely inadequate. Their night-sights were poor and they were unable to calculate angles of attack accurately. On top of that, crews were inexperienced and made numerous errors of judgement. One submarine commander carried out four patrols without sinking a single vessel, due to firing from too great a distance.

In late April the tide began to turn. The same officer who had failed so spectacularly in his previous four missions, Lieutenant Commander David Wanklyn, was warned that he had one last

An impressive line of Italian destroyers in the harbour at Naples as Mussolini demonstrates Italy's massed naval strength to the visiting Hitler.

chance to redeem himself. After setting out on 21 April, on 25 April he sighted and sank a merchant ship. Later that month he boarded a ship that had run aground and set it on fire. Then on 1 May he attacked a convoy protected by four destroyers and sank two merchant ships. He returned to Malta flying the Jolly Roger, as was the custom for British sailors in the Mediterranean.

In May, Wanklyn enjoyed mixed fortunes. First he fired a wild salvo at a convoy on 15 May from 7,000 yards (4 miles, 6.4 km) and hit nothing and then on 24 May he sighted a troop convoy bound for North Africa. His sound detection apparatus was not functioning and so it was not until his final periscope observation that he saw a destroyer near his boat. He quickly submerged and resurfaced to attack one of the ships. Four torpedoes were fired and the troopship was hit.

The convoy counter-attacked with 37 depth charges but none hit the target. When the submarine resurfaced two hours later the convoy had sailed away. However, the *Conte Rosso* had been sunk and nearly half of the 3,000 Italian soldiers on board had been killed. After a shaky start, Wanklyn became the top British submarine 'ace'.[10]

THE SIEGE OF MALTA

The Italian declaration of war in 1940 and the fall of France created huge logistical problems for British shipping. It was no longer safe for them to enter the Mediterranean and instead they were forced to sail the long route via the Cape of Good Hope and round the Horn of Africa to Suez. This added thousands of miles and an enormous amount of time, with journeys taking as much as three months. A vast quantity of extra fuel was also used, which took its toll on the supply chain. On the other hand, Italy and Germany could easily supply their troops via the short distance from Italian ports to Tripoli and Benghazi.

Malta was a crucial outpost for Britain in the Mediterranean and the only reasonable point from which the British could attack Axis supply lines. Its position, midway between Sicily and North Africa, meant it could directly influence the North African campaign and pressurize Italy. As a result, the island's key strategic role made it a target for some of the most sustained attacks by Axis forces. It was blockaded and subjected to aerial bombardment in an attempt to cut off its supplies and ultimately starve it into surrender.

From January 1941, the Italians, supported by the Luftwaffe, began an intensive bombing campaign against the island. Malta had been attacked by Italian bombers shortly after its declaration of war and in 1940 the island was poorly defended, with only a small contingent of Gloster Gladiator biplanes and a handful of anti-aircraft guns available for defence. If the Italians had launched a full-scale invasion of Malta at that point it would have fallen, with incalculable consequences for the British war effort.

The raid motivated the British to send over Hawker Hurricanes to protect the island and reinforce its defences. However, the Italian assault on Malta was not followed up by significant military or aerial activity, so the British had time to prepare for the next onslaught.

Even so, it was difficult for the British to defend Malta adequately and keep it supplied. The facilities for repairing aircraft were limited and spare parts were not easily available. Fuel was also a precious resource, which was difficult to transport to the island.

In November 1940 an aircraft carrier sailed from Gibraltar with 12 Hurricanes on board, but only four were delivered successfully to Malta with the rest lost at sea. This represented a setback for the Allies, as there was only a primitive radar system on the island and RAF pilots were always outnumbered.

However, once German Messerschmitts arrived they were also at a disadvantage, this time in terms of speed and height.[11]

CHURCHILL'S GAMBLE

The war in North Africa was going so badly for the British that Churchill overrode the furious objections of his chiefs of staff and ordered a convoy carrying over 300 tanks to sail to Alexandria through the Mediterranean route. The convoy would be exposed to attacks from aircraft and submarines, but if it completed the journey successfully it would enable the tanks to be delivered two months earlier than sailing via the Cape and the Horn of Africa.

Two aircraft carriers, including the *Ark Royal*, accompanied the transport vessels. On 12 May the convoy reached its destination, having beaten off enemy attacks. Only one merchant ship was lost, together with its cargo of 57 tanks. Churchill's gamble had succeeded. If it had failed, it could have cost the war and would certainly have led to defeat in North Africa. However, its success bought time and enabled the British and Commonwealth forces to continue fighting.[12]

THE SIEGE OF MALTA INTENSIFIES

Following the German conquest of Crete, the Axis powers launched a renewed attack upon Malta. The naval blockade of the island had been so successful that between January and April 1941 it had become impossible for British ships to reach Malta. By April 1942 the situation was so desperate that the island's governor sent a telegram to London informing them that 'the very worst may happen if we cannot replenish our vital needs, especially flour and ammunition'.[13]

The island was subjected to a devastating aerial bombardment, with German and Italian planes dropping 6,500 tons

(5,900 tonnes) of bombs. Valletta, the capital, received nearly half of the bombload and the onslaught led to hundreds of deaths and virtually destroyed the port, compelling the Royal Navy to retreat to Alexandria. Malta was bombed more heavily than London during the height of the Blitz.

The result of the naval blockade and the bombing raids was to make it virtually impossible to prevent supplies from being delivered to the Germans and Italians in North Africa. By April nearly 90 per cent of the required supplies were reaching the Axis forces and Rommel was preparing to launch an invasion of Egypt. Every attempt by British convoys to break through the naval blockade and resupply the island failed. Axis superiority in the air and at sea was too great.

By early August the situation was so desperate that Churchill, aware of the consequences of the loss of Malta, decided on a desperate plan to rescue the island from imminent surrender. He knew its chances of success were slim and that it would involve heavy casualties which, in the event of failure, might lead to the loss of the Battle of the Mediterranean, but felt that inaction would bring about certain defeat.[14]

OPERATION PEDESTAL

On 2 August 1942, 14 merchant ships sailed from the River Clyde en route to Malta. The carefully planned attempt to deliver crucial supplies to the stricken island was named Operation Pedestal. They were protected by seven cruisers, three aircraft carriers, two battleships and 32 destroyers. Six submarines were also asked to patrol the sea between Sicily and the coast of Tunisia, another submarine was placed to the west of Palermo and an eighth boat was sent to guard the Strait of Messina.

On 10 August the convoy reached Gibraltar, where it was joined by a third aircraft carrier, HMS *Furious*, containing

A view of Valletta in Malta showing its harbour filled with British naval hardware, 1941.

38 Supermarine Spitfires for delivery to Malta. They arrived at Gibraltar in thick fog and the following day began their perilous journey. Next morning the convoy was spotted by reconnaissance planes and *Furious* began flying off the Spitfires. The convoy was then detected by *U-73*, which attacked the aircraft carrier HMS *Eagle* and hit it with all four torpedoes. *Eagle* sank within eight minutes.

That evening *Furious* returned to Gibraltar. German planes attacked the convoy, but none of the bombs hit their target. Next morning, they resumed their attack and one merchant ship was damaged. That same evening the remaining carrier was severely damaged and a destroyer was sunk. The convoy then lost its escort of heavy ships, which returned to Gibraltar, leaving four cruisers and the destroyers to guard the merchant ships from Sicily and Tunisia to Malta.

As the convoy approached Tunis, 13 Italian submarines were lying in wait. Torpedoes struck a cruiser, the escort's flagship and the oil tanker *Ohio*. The cruiser sank and the flagship was forced to return to Gibraltar for repairs. The convoy was then attacked by German aircraft and two merchant ships were sunk and another was damaged.

Another group of Italian submarines hit a third cruiser and damaged it and two more merchant ships were sunk. The following day a group of German and Italian torpedo boats knocked out another cruiser and a merchant ship and sank four merchantmen. The damaged cruiser's captain was forced to scuttle the ship.

Later that morning the remaining ships, 50 miles (80 km) behind their original schedule, were being protected by Bristol Beaufighters from Malta but as the convoy drew closer German bombers attacked again in force. One merchant ship was sunk and the tanker *Ohio* was further damaged. Three hours later more bombers attacked, setting another merchant ship on fire and causing further damage to another ship and the *Ohio*.

Throughout the convoy's journey the *Ohio* was singled out for attack by the Axis forces. Its precious cargo of fuel was too valuable for them to allow it to enter Valletta harbour. The ship was hit with torpedoes and holed repeatedly, causing fire to break out on board followed by engine failure and exploding boilers. Twice the crew abandoned the ship and twice they reboarded it. A number of attempts were made to tow the *Ohio* and none were successful, but in spite of its damage the ship refused to sink. The sailors on board the tanker fought to keep it afloat and were exhausted by the time it arrived in port, having had no rest or sleep during the relentless bombardment of the vessel.

The first ship to reach Malta was the *Rochester Castle*, which was hit in its hold by two torpedoes but managed to stay afloat and limp into port at 6.15 p.m. on 13 August, followed by the *Melbourne Star* and *Port Chalmers*. The wounded were landed at Sliema by motor launches which proceeded to assist the other ships, particularly the vital but desperately damaged *Ohio*.[15]

The *Rochester Castle* was so badly stricken by the sustained assault upon it that it was compelled to stay in Malta until December, when it made a dangerous journey to Alexandria and then New York, via the Cape of Good Hope, where it was repaired. Following its repairs it sailed to Argentina, returning in June 1943 with a cargo of frozen meat. However, two of the surviving merchant ships were so badly damaged that they were no longer serviceable.[16]

The cost of Operation Pedestal was huge. Beaufighters and Spitfires had flown over 400 sorties to protect the convoy, while the Royal Navy lost two cruisers, an aircraft carrier and a destroyer. In addition, two other cruisers and another carrier were badly damaged. The Italians lost just two submarines. There were some isolated British successes, though. In a separate part of the operation a British submarine damaged two cruisers so badly that they were unable to continue in active service.

Although Operation Pedestal did not end the pressure on Malta it did enough to save it from imminent collapse, so Churchill's desperate gamble had paid off.[17]

MALTA AFTER PEDESTAL

Operation Pedestal was a temporary respite for Malta but the naval blockade and aerial onslaught on the island continued. Following the successful delivery of supplies Malta's Beaufort bombers began to attack German and Italian supply lines.[18] They were soon joined by a new complement of British submarines.[19]

The Germans responded by intensifying aerial attacks and more British submarines were sent to reinforce the island's defences. One British submariner described everyday life on the island:

> No food. No spares. Incessant bombing, submarines being repaired by half-starved Maltese workmen in inadequate shelters hand-scooped out of rock around the harbour. It was amazing that any base could function at all, much less continue delivering blows at the enemy.[20]

This situation improved dramatically during mid-October 1942, when Malta's Spitfires destroyed 131 Axis planes and lost only 34 aircraft. This rate of attrition forced the Germans and Italians to abandon the attempt to bomb the island into submission.[21]

A German submarine ties up at a naval base in Italy, January 1943.

The military victory did not compensate for the desperate shortage of food, fuel and weapons, however, and a relief operation codenamed 'Stoneage' was launched to resupply the island. On 17 November a convoy containing four merchant ships escorted by destroyers and cruisers sailed from Alexandria. It had air cover until it came near to the island, at which point Beaufighters and Spitfires took over the aerial protection role.

The convoy entered Valletta successfully, with one cruiser damaged but all four merchant ships unharmed. On its entry to the harbour cheering crowds welcomed it. The arrival of the convoy, along with the collapse of the Axis forces in North Africa and the growing war-weariness among the Italians, saved Malta. It was a decisive turning point in the Battle of the Mediterranean.[22]

THE FRENCH FLEET SCUTTLES ITSELF

On 27 November 1942 Germany decided to seize the French fleet in Toulon. When the Germans attacked the French decided to scuttle their ships rather than let them fall into German hands, though four French submarines escaped and joined the Allies. Over 50 ships and 14 submarines were destroyed and only 39 French ships fell into German hands. This was a major blow to Axis attempts to seize control of the Mediterranean, particularly given the size and strength of the French navy.[23]

BRITISH SUBMARINES FIGHT BACK

British submarines had a lean time of it for a while because Italian escorts had been fitted with better detection equipment and some ships were routed further east to Tobruk. However, the boats enjoyed a rare success in October. Five submarines lay in wait for a convoy bound for Tripoli, planning to ambush it, and the successful submarine sank a merchant ship and a destroyer before its presence was detected by a seaplane and a destroyer and it was forced to submerge. The boat also damaged an oil tanker, though that still managed to reach port with two other merchant ships.[24]

A combination of continuing submarine attacks and aircraft deployed from Egypt sank shipping to such an extent that the Italians were compelled to re-route their convoys via Benghazi and Tripoli. This created difficulties for Rommel as these ports were a considerable distance from his supply lines, which added to his existing problems with growing shortages of fuel, weapons and other necessities.

Operation Torch, involving British and American troops with new tanks and anti-aircraft guns, saw a force commanded by Eisenhower land in Morocco and Algeria. Coupled with Montgomery's attack from the east, it was designed to drive the Germans and Italians out of Africa altogether.

Torch came as a complete surprise to the Axis forces. They quickly assembled a fleet of German and Italian submarines in an attempt to attack Allied supply lines around the Strait of Gibraltar and on 11 November *U-407* sank the troopship *Viceroy of India*. The same day *U-380* sank a Dutch liner. By contrast November saw three Italian submarines and five U-boats sunk while in December another four Italian submarines were lost. In mid-November British submarines were based around Tunis and Bizerte. They harried the Axis supply lines relentlessly and made reinforcing their troops in North Africa increasingly difficult.[25]

By February 1943 British submarines sank over 40,000 tons of Axis shipping. Only 20 per cent of German supplies were getting through to North Africa by April and fuel shortages became so acute that by May the Axis forces were compelled to surrender. Nearly all Axis shipping had been destroyed and the German army fought on alone with dwindling resources. British submarines had sunk 29 per cent of Axis shipping in the Mediterranean, which represented a remarkable turnaround from the poor showing they had made up to then.[26]

U-331 was the last U-boat sunk during Operation Torch, after being bombed by three RAF planes. The crew tried to surrender, but at that point a naval unit attacked the survivors before a destroyer and a flying boat arrived and rescued them. By that time only 17 were still alive. Torch was a disaster for the U-boats involved in fighting the Allies.[27]

U-BOATS ON THE DEFENSIVE

The Mediterranean was now effectively under Allied control and the Suez Canal was fully open for traffic. Naval and air superiority made it difficult for U-boats to attack successfully and from now on the U-boats fought an entirely defensive war. The days of attacking shipping were all but over and the naval battle for the Germans entirely focused on survival.

On 4 June a flotilla of U-boats attacked Convoy KMS-18D, which was designed to be part of the group invading Sicily. The wolfpack sank six ships and damaged three others. This was the last major offensive action by German U-boats in Mediterranean waters.[28]

On 10 June the Allies invaded Sicily in a huge operation involving troopships and supply vessels. Twelve days passed before two U-boats attacked two ships, both of which were damaged but remained afloat. However, three U-boats were sunk by the Allies.

The Italian government was in crisis and the fleet refused to attack. Hitler asked Dönitz if he believed that sending more U-boats to the Mediterranean would assist the situation. Dönitz responded that he thought it would make little difference and would be difficult given the Allied control of the Strait of Gibraltar.

In spite of Dönitz's objections three U-boats were sent to reinforce the naval capacity, but none were able to reach the Mediterranean and all were destroyed. On 21 August *U-458* sank an American ship but two destroyers in the convoy then sank the U-boat. The total success rate in August was three merchant ships sunk and another damaged for the loss of four U-boats, an unsustainable rate of destruction.[29]

After the Allies had achieved complete naval and air supremacy, the U-boat war became a series of sporadic attacks rather than a sustained campaign. When Mussolini was deposed in July 1943 Dönitz ordered the navy to seize the Italian fleet in its ports of La Spezia, Taranto and Genoa and capture all Italian merchant ships.

However, the new Italian government, suspecting German intentions, tried to prevent their fleet from falling into German hands. They lied to Kesselring and promised that the fleet would sail out to meet the Allies and fight them to the death, but they had no intention of fighting and their real objective was to sail to Malta and surrender their navy to the Allies.

Once the Germans grasped the Italian plan they tried to attack the navy and four vessels were destroyed. Nevertheless, the bulk of the fleet reached Malta safely and surrendered. It was a devastating blow for German hopes of a Mediterranean counter-attack.[30]

Following the Italian surrender, the U-boat fleet in the Mediterranean was reduced to 13 boats available for action. In September they sank seven ships, five of them merchantmen, and damaged two more ships for the loss of one U-boat. Dönitz ordered seven submarines to be sent from the Atlantic to reinforce the boats in the Mediterranean, but only one managed to break through the Allied cordon. Another was damaged and the rest were unable to pass.

In the end, Dönitz was forced to abandon the attempt at relief, so the 13 submarines would have to fend for themselves against overwhelming odds.[31]

U-223 was the only U-boat to enter the Mediterranean successfully, when it damaged a tramp steamer but did not sink it. One of the U-boats already stationed there then sank a freighter and an oil tanker.

The invasion of Sicily led to the sinking of an American destroyer, a Norwegian tanker and a minesweeper-destroyer, while another ship was damaged. Three U-boats were lost during the campaign.

November saw one ship and one Allied submarine sunk and another ship damaged and in December four ships were sunk and one U-boat was lost. Only 13 submarines now remained in the Mediterranean.

In 1944 the U-boats enjoyed isolated successes but far greater losses, in an increasingly hopeless struggle. By August no more U-boats could operate from liberated southern France and by October the bases in Greece were abandoned.[32]

During the Battle of the Mediterranean U-boats sank over 100 vessels totalling in excess of half a million tons. There were never enough U-boats available, however, and the Mediterranean was a difficult area of operations. British control of Gibraltar proved crucial in denying German submarines access to the region. If Hitler had devoted more military and air resources to the conflict Britain might have been defeated, but U-boats alone were never capable of controlling the Mediterranean.

NOTES

1   BdU KTB, 5 December 1939, quoted in Lawrence Paterson, *U-Boats in the Mediterranean, 1941–1944*, Chatham Publishing, 2007
2   Paterson, op. cit.
3   Ibid.
4   Ibid.
5   Ibid.
6   Churchill, *The Second World War*, vol. 3
7   http://michaeltfassbender.com/nonfiction/the-world-wars/battles-and-campaigns/the-mediterranean-u-boat-campaign-1940-1943/
8   Arthur Hezlet, *The Submarine and Sea Power*, Peter Davis, 1967
9   F.H. Kinsley and Alan Stripp, *Codebreakers: The Inside Story of Bletchley Park*, Oxford University Press, 1993
10 James Allaway, *Hero of the Upholder: Lt-Cdr. M. D. Wanklyn VC DSO, The Royal Navy's Top Submarine Ace*, Airlife, 1991
11 Padfield, *War Beneath the Sea*
12 Dimbleby, op. cit.
13 Ibid.
14 Churchill, *The Hinge of Fate*
15 Dimbleby, op. cit.
16 Philip Vella, *Malta: Blitzed But Not Defeated*, Progress Press, 1997
17 http://www.naval-history.net/xAH-MaltaSupply01.htm/
18 Dimbleby, op. cit.
19 James Douglas-Hamilton, *The Air Battle for Malta*, Airlife, 1981
20 Alistair Mars, *British Submarines at War 1939–1945*, William Kimber, 1971
21 King, op. cit.
22 Tony Spooner, *Supreme Gallantry: Malta's Role in the Allied Victory, 1939–1945*, John Murray, 1996
23 King, op. cit.
24 John Jordan and Stephen Dent (editors), *Warship 2013*, Conway, 2013
25 Mars, op. cit.
26 Padfield, *War Beneath the Waves*
27 Admiral of the Fleet Viscount Cunningham, *A Sailor's Odyssey*, Hutchinson, 1951
28 Paterson, op. cit.
29 Ibid.
30 Ibid.
31 Ibid.
32 Ibid.

CHAPTER SEVEN

THE ARCTIC CONVOYS

The Arctic convoy campaign was the last great naval war. It was a conflict in which German deficiencies – both technical and strategic – played a part in the eventual victory of the Allies.[1]

The journey to north Russia meant convoys sailing to within 750 miles (1,200 km) of the North Pole and they faced temperatures as low as -50°C (-58°F) degrees. Even on arrival, ships disembarking at Murmansk or Archangel found themselves weighed down not simply by their cargo, but by a massive load of up to 150 tons (136 tonnes) of ice.

Floating pack ice made conditions difficult for combat vessels and merchant ships alike. Ships frequently became stuck in the ice, and were either damaged by it or so weighed down by its mass that they capsized. In the winter the White Sea froze over and it was impossible to approach Archangel, because ice blocked every entrance to the port. Icebergs, particularly the submerged type nicknamed 'growlers', were treacherous obstacles to ships attempting passage and nights were a thick pall of darkness, even when there was no fog obscuring the sky. There were frequent snowfalls and harsh winds lashed at the sailors. When the cold was at its most extreme, food and water on board the ships froze into ice. In the Arctic the chances of survival were small in the winter months and men whose vessels were hit generally died of hypothermia in the freezing waters.

It was equally challenging for the U-boats, whose crews found it difficult to operate in either summer or winter. In the summer there was perpetual sunshine which made it almost impossible for U-boats to attack without being detected, particularly on the only stretch of coastline that stayed ice-free all year round, the Kola Peninsula and Murmansk, due to its proximity to the Gulf Stream. Daylight brought its own difficulties but in the dark winter months it was hard for U-boats to operate because without other means of detecting targets such as reconnaissance aircraft their task was extremely demanding. The hostile coastline made it easy for Russian ships to conceal themselves while it was nearly impossible for U-boats to remain hidden. Even when they launched their torpedoes the shallow water of the peninsula often meant that they did not fire effectively.

U-boat crews could not even take advantage of the limited facilities for hospitality open to Allied sailors. Royal Navy seamen were able to leave almost as soon as they finished escorting the convoys, though the merchantmen were often laid up for months in port. This led to problems ranging from boredom and drunkenness to even fighting. The paranoid reluctance of Russians to 'fraternize' with Western sailors added to the frustration of the men. Prostitution was rare and mainly took the form of married women whose husbands were away fighting allowing merchant sailors to have sex in return for chocolate or cigarettes.[2]

Nearly 2,000 naval personnel and 829 merchant seamen lost their lives delivering goods to Russia. Many pilots on both sides, as well as submarine crews, also died in action – most of the latter were on German U-boats, though some British and Soviet submariners also perished at sea.[3]

GERMANY'S INVASION OF THE SOVIET UNION

From the beginning of the convoys in June 1941 until their eventual end in May 1945 the death toll on the Arctic run was horrific. One in every 20 merchant ships to Russia was sunk, 104 ships in total being lost. Added to that, the Royal Navy lost 22 ships and the German navy lost four ships and 31 U-boats. Both Allied and German crews suffered higher casualties than in the Atlantic because the Arctic winter magnified the ordinary dangers of war and resulted in a higher rate of fatalities than in less extreme conditions.

The Arctic convoys arose following the German invasion of the Soviet Union on 22 June 1941. This led to an immediate if uneasy alliance between Britain and Russia. Churchill was under no illusion about Stalin and complained that he regarded the fall of France with 'stony composure' and refused to support British attempts 'to create a front in the Balkans'.[4] Another point of contention between them was the active assistance the Russians had given to Germany, both in terms of supplies and refuelling facilities. The general view was that Stalin wanted Britain to lose the war so that he could dismantle the British Empire and bring at least some of its countries under Soviet domination or even occupation. On the Russian side, most Soviet leaders – Stalin is one of the few exceptions – expected the Germans to turn on them and focused their energies on making the nation as strong as possible when the invasion was launched. It is remarkable, therefore, that such a devious man was taken by surprise when the Germans invaded and for a few days remained in a state of shock and was unable to function.

Now they were under attack the situation changed. In Churchill's words: 'The Soviet Union's first impulse and lasting policy was to demand all possible succour from Great Britain and her Empire.'[5]

Stalin was equally dismissive of the British. He regarded the North African campaign as an irrelevant diversion and had no understanding of the importance of the naval war. That failure to grasp naval strategy and tactics remained with him throughout the conflict and was a major handicap to Russian endeavours.

Once the Soviet Union was under attack, Stalin demanded that Britain should launch an immediate invasion of France and that American supplies destined for Britain should instead be diverted to Russia. Both ideas were completely unrealistic and Churchill was forced to explain to Stalin that it would be impossible for him to comply.

DECISION TO SEND CONVOYS

Instead he offered 'naval and air operations' to support and supply the Russians through Arctic convoys. Churchill's proposal raised furious objections from Admiral Pound but he pressed ahead, insisting on the importance of keeping Russia in the war.

On 1 August 1941 the British cruiser HMS *Adventure* docked at Archangel, carrying a cargo of military supplies including mines and between 10 and 15 September Russian destroyers laid the British mines, in spite of their complaints that they were 'unsuitable'. The British agreed to send regular convoys to the Soviet Union, though less frequently than Stalin demanded, and it was decided that during the winter months the destination port would be Murmansk rather than Archangel.

Rear Admiral Philip Vian, the British naval officer who had been asked to liaise with his Russian counterpart, had considerable reservations about the suitability of Murmansk as a port. For a start, it was too close to the air base at Petsamo, which was under German occupation, and Murmansk had already been heavily bombed. The port facilities were basic and anti-aircraft defences poor and the railway line between Murmansk and Leningrad had been severed by the Germans. Although the Russians were relaying the track it created problems in transporting supplies.[6]

All merchant ships arriving at the port would be compelled to remain at anchor in Vaenga Bay, where they were vulnerable to air attack. To make the port serviceable would require considerable construction work and a permanent British naval presence to assist the Russians.[7]

In spite of these deficiencies Churchill insisted on sending convoys to Murmansk. He knew that British resources were already stretched and so he approached Roosevelt for help. The president agreed to send supplies to Russia, though he stressed that the transportation of these supplies remained a British responsibility.

As expected, the Germans launched attacks on Murmansk from their bases in Norway and the British sent submarines to counter them. They had some success in sinking German ships but they were inadequate to deal with the Axis threat unaided. The German bases in Norway, on the other hand, were well-equipped and ships, aircraft and U-boats operated out of them effectively. And as those on Arctic convoy duty discovered, the winter months were intensely cold and during the summer the perpetual daylight presented problems. It was not clear that British convoy ships would be capable of overcoming these hazards and be able to deliver the necessary supplies to the Russians.[8]

Before the decision to begin despatching convoys to Murmansk was taken Vian was asked to examine a possible alternative location. Spitsbergen, though part of Norway, was a bleak and inhospitable island close to Russia, but the Germans had not thought it worthwhile to occupy it or use it as a base

A De Havilland Mosquito FB Mark VI of 'A' Flight, No.143 Squadron, RAF Coastal Command, fires on two moored merchant vessels with rockets and cannons during an attack by the Banff Strike Wing on concentrations of enemy shipping in Sandefjord, Norway, April 1945.

for attacking the Soviet Union. Vian sailed there in the cruiser *Nigeria*, with two destroyers and another cruiser as his escort, but he rapidly decided that while Spitsbergen was relatively safe from German air raids it was too remote from Russia to be a suitable base. However, before he left he evacuated the Russian coal miners and the few remaining Norwegian personnel on the island, destroyed the coal mines and sailed to Archangel to disembark the Russians. He also captured six ships and two fishing boats.[9]

The first British convoy bound for Russia sailed from Hvalfiordur in Iceland on 21 August 1941. Its codename was Dervish and it was relatively small, comprising six merchant ships escorted by three destroyers, three minesweepers and three trawlers. Also accompanying the convoy was the aircraft carrier HMS *Argus*, which was loaded with 24 Hurricane aircraft. These were flown off and landed at Vaenga airfield. Fifteen more Hurricanes were stored in the hold of the cargo ships and were unpacked and assembled by 15 September. After ten days the convoy unloaded its supplies, which mainly consisted of rubber, tin and wool, at Archangel.[10]

BRITISH SUBMARINES ENTER THE ARCTIC WAR

In July Admiral Sir John Tovey, in charge of convoy operations, sent two British submarines to operate from the Kola base. Others followed with the mission of disrupting German shipping around Norway.

Both Churchill and Stalin were strategically naïve in terms of what the Arctic convoys could achieve. Stalin demanded that Soviet ice-breaking ships should keep the Arctic ports open throughout the year and Churchill promised to despatch convoys every ten days. It was impossible to meet either demand and while Churchill had angry exchanges with his naval chiefs,

Stalin accused both the British and his own people of deliberate sabotage.

Meanwhile, Operation Barbarossa progressed and though the German army was gaining ground the naval war was accomplishing little on either side. Raeder's warning to Hitler that the German failure to capture Murmansk might be a costly mistake was dismissed and Dönitz complained bitterly that the U-boats he had been compelled to send against the Russian ships 'found practically no targets and accomplished nothing worth mentioning'.[11]

British submarines were equally unsuccessful as they failed to encounter German shipping due to the fact that the Arctic weather made detection of enemy vessels difficult. Operating effectively was as much of a problem for them as it was for the Germans.

THE WAR AGAINST THE CONVOYS BEGINS
In 1941 the British convoys saw many dangers from the weather and surface vessels of the German navy, but on the whole they delivered supplies successfully. One ship was sunk by U-boats and another British ship was damaged, but that was the result of ice rather than enemy action.

On 1 January 1942 the merchant ship *Waziristan* loaded up military supplies for the Soviet Union and then sailed from New York, but it missed its designated escorts in poor weather. The following morning, in the seas between Norway and Russia, the *Waziristan* was struck by a torpedo fired by *U-134*. The vessel sank and 47 sailors died.

The first wolfpack attack on an Arctic convoy took place on 17 January. It was directed against convoy PQ-8, which comprised seven merchant ships escorted by two minesweepers, two destroyers and a cruiser. At 7.45 p.m. the convoy was attacked by *U-454*. There were three U-boats in this attack but only *U-454* was successful. A torpedo hit one of the merchant ships but the captain managed to save his vessel.

U-454 then loosed another salvo of torpedoes at an oil tanker in the convoy. They missed the target but struck the destroyer protecting the vessel. It caught fire rapidly and out of the 200 crew members only two survived. Around 50 managed to escape the sinking ship but they died of hypothermia in the freezing Arctic waters. This was the only casualty of the operation and most of the cargo was delivered safely.

SUBMARINE WAR

PQ-13 was the next convoy to come under successful attack by U-boats. Previous convoys had been damaged by ice, stormy weather, German aircraft and surface vessels, but the submarine war in the Arctic had been relatively ineffective. PQ-13 faced the same dangers of the hostile environment and German planes and ships but from this point onwards the U-boats began to intervene with deadly consequences.

There were 19 merchant ships in the convoy and an escort of two destroyers and three armed trawlers. It left Iceland on 20 March and immediately ran into freezing temperatures and gale force winds. For four days the storm lashed the ships and then on 27 March it finally ceased, but by that time the convoy had been scattered far and wide. Some ships were as distant as 150 miles (240 km) from the main convoy group.[12]

The appalling weather was a precursor to an even more dangerous ordeal. PQ-13 was detected by a German reconnaissance plane and found itself under attack from bombers, surface ships and U-boats. Two ships were sunk by German aircraft and three destroyers sank another vessel, before they were in turn attacked by British warships. The destroyer *Trinidad* inflicted severe damage on a German destroyer using its guns and then tried to finish the enemy ship off by firing its torpedoes. However, a bizarre gyro malfunction meant that the one torpedo to successfully leave the ship made a U-turn and instead struck the British destroyer. She was able to crawl her way into Kola inlet with an escort in spite of this disastrous accident.[13] Meanwhile, the German destroyer was sunk after other ships joined in the attack.

The other ships in the convoy were also attacked by U-boats, with two ships being sunk. Although the warships tried to fight back and believed mistakenly that they had sunk a U-boat, later it was discovered that the submarine had been sunk in another battle.[14]

By 30 March the majority of the convoys had reached Murmansk, with the final vessels arriving on 1 April. Six ships were destroyed during the convoy's journey, five of them freighters, another ship had been lost through the icy conditions and *Trinidad* was damaged. On the Axis side a single German destroyer had been sunk. Fourteen ships arrived in Murmansk, but a third of the original contingent was lost.[15]

BIG DECISION

PQ-17 was the largest convoy that had ever been sent out to sea. It was also the first major exercise in joint Anglo-American naval transport. It left Iceland on 27 June 1942 and prepared to sail to the Soviet Arctic ports of Archangel and Murmansk. There were 35 ships in the convoy and 26 warships sailed with it to protect it from German attack.

On 4 July the Germans began to attack the convoy with Heinkel bombers. Three merchant ships were hit, but German planes were also downed. The attack on the convoy raised alarm bells in the Admiralty and Pound was asked to take a decision about the mission. He considered ordering the convoy to turn

Soviet warships escorting convoys delivering aid to the Soviet Union repel a German air attack in the Barents Sea, 1942.

back but eventually decided to remove the protective cruisers instead. After taking that decision he commanded the convoy to scatter and make its way to Russia as individual units rather than a group. Following this, the remaining British warships abandoned the convoy.

Twelve U-boats and over 100 German bombers then attacked the defenceless merchant ships and 12 merchantmen were lost in the first 24 hours. Although he was quickly informed of the situation, Pound did not countermand his orders. Instead, he allowed the unprotected convoy to continue on its doomed journey without any kind of shield from aircraft or surface vessels.

The result was utter devastation for the merchant ships. Many had already become widely separated by the weather and Pound's order meant that the majority of them were now lone ships facing an unremitting onslaught from the Luftwaffe, German surface ships and U-boats.

There is no doubt that fear of the giant battleship *Tirpitz* also played its part. This German ship was the largest and most powerful warship in the world and was berthed in Norway. The Admiralty believed that it was on the move from its base and was preparing to attack the convoy and prevent it from reaching Russia with its supplies.

In fact, *Tirpitz* had left its base at Trondheim but was engaged in manoeuvres and had not yet set out to pursue Allied shipping. Such intelligence as was available to the British showed that it was not an immediate threat to the convoy and that information should have been sufficient for the ships to continue to receive naval protection.

Air cover was impossible with the Germans in control of Norway and RAF planes unable to operate effectively at such a distance from Britain. The only possible form of protection for the merchant ships was the Royal Navy and it had been instructed by Pound to withdraw. The effect of this order, based on the mistaken idea that the *Tirpitz* was about to launch an imminent attack, was exacerbated by his extraordinary decision to instruct the convoy to scatter.

FAILED BRITISH PLAN

Bad intelligence was compounded by a dangerous and, as events proved, unworkable plan to lure the German fleet out of its Norwegian bases so that the Royal Navy and the RAF could attempt to destroy it. There were two parts to the attempted deception and the first part failed completely. A double agent fed false information to the Germans about two convoys, one leaving from Iceland and the other from Scapa Flow. It was reported that the missions of both convoys were to transport troops for an attack on Norway. However, the convoy leaving Scapa Flow was a decoy consisting totally of armed ships.

The Germans believed this false intelligence and began to collect a large force of surface ships, aircraft and U-boats to sink the two convoys. Their operation was given the codename *Rösselsprung* – 'Knight's Move' – and was planned to involve not only the *Tirpitz* but also the pocket battleships *Admiral Scheer* and *Lützow* and the cruiser *Admiral Hipper*, together with a small group of destroyers from Trondheim.

It was planned to attack convoy PQ-17 east of Bear Island, operating in close reach of the Norwegian coast and supported by aircraft and U-boats. The Allies attempted to counter this strategy, but they had no air cover and were so short of fuel that they would be unable to escort a damaged ship to a safe harbour.

Realizing their weakness if Rösselsprung was launched successfully, the Admiralty ordered the convoy to retreat if there was a danger of imminent German attack. They also declared that surface ships would only protect the convoy to the west of Bear Island, while east of that they would have to rely on British submarines.

Two events conspired to make the British plans unworkable. One was that the Germans delayed their attacks longer than expected and the other was that the dummy convoy was not even detected by German reconnaissance aircraft so no ships or U-boats were lured out to attack it.

CATASTROPHIC ORDERS FROM THE ADMIRALTY

PQ-17, by contrast, was detected as soon as it entered hostile waters and was stalked by *U-456* and then by Luftwaffe planes. A failed attack on the convoy was launched on 2 July, but it inflicted no damage and resulted in the loss of a plane. Then on 4 July an aircraft bombed a merchant ship, which had to be scuttled by the escorting warships. Later that day six bombers attacked again but the attack was beaten off. In the evening 25 bombers attacked the convoy and sank another ship for the loss of three aircraft.

A series of confusing messages from the Admiralty was then sent to the escorting ships. First they ordered the protecting warships to withdraw to the west and then a later message was sent ordering the convoy to scatter. The impression gained by the Royal Navy officers in charge was that an attack by the *Tirpitz* was expected imminently. That was the false intelligence on which the orders given by the Admiralty were based, but it was completely untrue. The *Tirpitz* had sailed out of its base but it was not preparing to attack the convoy.

By the time the instruction to scatter was received the convoy had already lost three ships. Spread out over a vast area and already separated by the weather, the vessels were now robbed of their naval protection and were expected to make their way through hostile conditions and enemy attacks entirely unaided. On 5 July six merchant ships were sunk by German aircraft and a further six by U-boats. Next day two more merchantmen were destroyed and on 7–8 July five other vessels were also sunk, two by U-boats. On 10 July two more ships were lost.

In spite of the order to abandon the convoy to its fate, Lieutenant Leo Gradwell, in charge of an armed trawler – a converted fishing boat – decided to defy his instructions. Gradwell took the view that as he was already in the region of the northern Arctic ice shelf there was no good reason why he should not escort the merchant ships. He persuaded three American merchant ships who were planning to retreat that he would protect them if they joined with him in delivering the supplies to Russia.

An epic journey followed in the course of which Gradwell ordered the ships to be painted white and the decks covered with white cloth to blend in with the Arctic ice and snow and so deceive the Germans. The Sherman tanks on the decks of the merchant ships were then arranged in a defensive formation with their guns loaded.

Although the four ships remained stuck in the Arctic ice pack for some time, their deceptive ruse was successful. They evaded detection by the Luftwaffe and were able to proceed to the Matochkin Strait, where a small flotilla of corvettes discovered them. These welcome allies escorted Gradwell's convoy and two other merchant ships safely into Archangel on 25 July.

Thirty-five merchant ships had set sail on their journey to Russia and 24 of them were sunk by aircraft or U-boats. It was the worst convoy disaster in the Second World War and ever since the reasoning behind Pound's order has been disputed.

The loss of life and the destruction of invaluable supplies was catastrophic and the Americans and the Russians were almost equally furious. Admiral King, already an Anglophobe, refused to send a waiting US convoy to the Soviet Union and instead diverted it to the Pacific and Stalin accused the British of deliberate sabotage.

As a result, Churchill was forced to suspend the Arctic convoys altogether and not until September did another set of merchant ships sail to the Soviet Union. This time they were thoroughly protected. The disaster of PQ-17 had military, economic, political and most of all human consequences and throughout the war the merchant seamen harboured fierce resentment towards the Royal Navy because of its abandonment of them, which made the relationship between the two branches poisonous. The whole disaster arose out of mistaken intelligence and an unwarranted fear of the *Tirpitz*, but it could so easily have been a triumph rather than one of the worst catastrophes in the history of naval warfare.[16]

LESSONS LEARNT

The devastating losses of life and cargo in convoy PQ-17 forced a radical rethink in naval strategy and when the next Arctic convoy, PQ-18, set sail its 40 merchant ships were provided with an escort of over 30 warships. These included 14 destroyers, four trawlers, two tankers, one cruiser and a salvage ship. However, this high degree of protection did not prevent a horrific rate of attrition and one third of the merchant ships were lost, some to aircraft and others to U-boats.

Convoy PQ-18 left Loch Ewe in Scotland on 2 September 1942 and it then rendezvoused with other ships and escorting vessels at Iceland before leaving on its journey to Russia. This was the first Arctic convoy to be accompanied by an aircraft carrier. Intelligence experts on both sides were busy reading the others' signals. Bletchley Park provided Ultra decryptions and the B-Dienst also read the British naval codes. The result was that the Germans had time to prepare their attacks, particularly with the suspension of Arctic convoys after the PQ-17 disaster.

On 12 September the assault on the convoy began. Bombers, U-boats, mines and torpedo bombers all played their part and 13 ships were sunk. It was a devastating total, but the rate of attrition was greater on the German side, with 44 aircraft and four U-boats lost.

On 16 September the convoy neared Archangel and its escorts were transferred to convoy QP-14, returning home from the Soviet Union. It was lashed by a storm which grounded several ships, though all were eventually refloated, and further attacks by the Luftwaffe were beaten off before the convoy eventually reached its destination on 21 September.

The ships delivered 150,000 tons (136,000 tonnes) of supplies to Archangel, which was the same amount as the entire cargo delivered to Russia in 1941.[17] It took a month to unload the supplies.

The losses on the Allied side were horrific and it was a victory in terms of political will and defiance, but the level of casualties was unsustainable. If the Luftwaffe had not been so badly damaged that its fighting capability in the area was greatly reduced the convoy would have been nearly as unsuccessful as PQ-17.

January 1943 saw the tide begin to turn in the Arctic battle. Convoy JW-51B came under sustained attack by the cruiser *Hipper* and the battleship *Lützow* but the escorting forces drove away the surface raiders. The heavy losses suffered by the Luftwaffe in their attacks on PQ-18 were compounded by the transfer of many Allied aircraft to the Mediterranean theatre, which assisted the safer running of convoys. Further successes were achieved when a Soviet submarine sank the steamer *Muansa* on 1 January 1943. However, *U-354* then sank the *Krasny Partizan*. Russian submarines achieved two more successes when they sank two German ships on 29 January, but *U-255* retaliated by sinking a Soviet icebreaker and a cargo ship. The same submarine also destroyed a merchant ship from convoy RA-52 on 3 February 1943.[18]

Following this, another Soviet submarine sank a German ship and on 26 February the last Allied convoy arrived at Kola Bay with only one ship damaged. On its arrival, four more ships were damaged by aircraft and one sank.

March saw three ships sunk by U-boats and then on 12 March the discovery that the *Tirpitz*, *Scharnhorst* and *Lützow* had gathered in Narvik, presumably with the intention of launching an offensive action against merchant ships or naval forces, led to the suspension of Arctic convoys.

Sporadic actions between U-boats and ships continued but convoy traffic did not resume until November 1943. In the meantime, on 8 September 1943 the *Tirpitz* and the *Scharnhorst*, accompanied by ten destroyers, launched a furious bombardment against Spitsbergen. But on 23 September a counter-strike by the Allies led to the *Tirpitz* becoming immobilized in Kåfjord and unable to proceed with further attacks.[19]

THE TURNING TIDE

In 1944, the convoys steadily established their supremacy as U-boats increasingly fought a losing battle. Greater air cover and more extensive and effective protection of merchant ships meant that the bulk of the supplies were now delivered successfully.

However, January saw U-boats sink four ships and damage another for the loss of one submarine, though a Russian submarine managed to sink a German ship.

In February, one Allied ship was sunk and one U-boat was destroyed, whereas March saw one ship sunk for the loss of three U-boats, turning the tables somewhat. In April five U-boats were lost and one merchant ship sunk and in May one U-boat was sunk and no ships were lost. There were no successes for the Germans in June or July and August saw two ships sunk and one damaged at the cost of two U-boats lost.

In early September, three minesweepers lent to the Russians by the Americans were sunk, together with a Soviet corvette, but only one merchant ship was lost and one U-boat was sunk by depth charges from a Russian minesweeper. Convoy RA-59's escorts sank another U-boat. Later that month two ships were sunk and one U-boat was lost. In October, no successful activity occurred, though November saw one convoy escort damaged and one ship sunk. In December, three ships were sunk and one U-boat was lost.

By 1945, the U-boat campaign was an exercise in defiance rather than an effective military strategy. Eleven ships were sunk and three U-boats were lost during the final five months of the war.

The final Arctic convoy battle of the war took place on 29 April, when convoy JW-66, comprising 22 merchant ships with a large escort, landed safely in the Kola Inlet. That day saw convoy RA-66 leave with its escort and 14 U-boats waiting off the coast came under attack. Two U-boats were sunk and a British frigate was torpedoed, with heavy casualties. The convoy arrived safely in Scotland on 8 May.

A final Russian convoy sailed after the German surrender. JW-67 left Scotland on 12 May with 23 merchant ships and arrived at Kola on 20 May. Three days later convoy RA-67 made the return journey and on 31 May reached its destination in Scotland. Were the rewards worth the ship losses, suffering and death? Opinions are divided on the issue. Some argue that a route via the Persian Gulf overland to Russia would have been safer and more effective at delivering supplies, while others claim that the goods transported made only a marginal difference to the outcome of the war.

There is little doubt that Stalin regarded the British and American ships delivering goods with deep suspicion. His insistence on the Arctic route to transport supplies has been seen as a deliberate attempt to destroy or at least fatally weaken the Royal Navy. Allied sailors were certainly treated badly once they reached the Soviet Union and Stalin's notorious paranoia led him to imagine that they would corrupt the Russians with their Western ways.

From 1943 it was obvious to everyone except Hitler that the Germans had been defeated by the Russians, but in 1941 and 1942 things were less clear-cut and a Nazi victory was entirely possible. With the fall of Communism and the subsequent collapse of the Soviet Union, Russian historians have been less parochial than before. They admit that without the vast quantities of weapons and raw materials sent to the Soviet Union during the first two years of the German–Soviet war the Russians would have been defeated. After 1943 the continuation of the convoys to Russia was a gesture of political support rather than being of vital military importance, but the evidence of the crucial years from 1941 to 1943 supports the idea that the Arctic convoys were an essential lifeline to the Soviet Union, without which it might have suffered defeat at the hands of the Nazis.

The Arctic convoy route was the cruellest of all missions undertaken by the Merchant Navy and the Royal Navy but it has neither been granted official status as an independent campaign nor have participants been issued with campaign medals. Surviving sailors of the Royal Navy and the Merchant Navy justifiably resent this snub, because without their heroic efforts the course of the war in Russia would have been very different. Russia, unlike America and Britain, has been more willing to recognize the contributions of the sailors on the Arctic convoys. There are memorials to the Allied dead, medals for those who served and visits by veterans to Murmansk and Archangel.

NOTES

1   Churchill, *Second World War, vol. III, The Grand Alliance*
2   Ibid.
3   Richard Woodman, *Arctic Convoys 1941–1945*, Pen and Sword, 1993
4   Ibid.
5   Ibid.
6   Ibid.
7   Ibid.
8   Ibid.
9   *Dönitz*, op. cit.
10 Woodman, op. cit.
11 Morris O. Mills, *Convoy PQ13: Unlucky for Some*, Bernard Durnford, 2000
12 Ibid.
13 Ibid.
14 Woodman, op. cit.
15 Ibid.
16 For varying accounts and interpretations of the PQ-17 disaster, the following books are recommended: Captain Jack Broome, *Convoy Is to Scatter*, William Kimber, 1972; David Irving, *The Destruction of PQ17*, Granada, 1985; P. Lund and H. Ludlam, *PQ17 – Convoy to Hell*, New English Library, 1969; Godfrey Winn, *PQ17: The Story of a Ship*, Universal Book Club, 1948. Broome and Winn were both directly involved with the PQ17 expedition.
17 Peter C. Smith, *Arctic Victory: Story of Convoy PQ18*, New English Library, 1977
18 Friedrich Ruge, *The Soviets as Naval Opponents, 1941–1945*, Naval Institute Press, 1979
19 Ibid.

CHAPTER EIGHT

THE WAR AT SEA IN AFRICAN AND ASIAN WATERS

The rapid decline in successful sinkings in the North Atlantic led the Germans to consider new areas of operation for their U-boats. Dönitz recognized that the convoy route between Cape Town and Freetown had increased in importance following the carnage in the Atlantic and saw new opportunities to destroy Allied merchant ships.

In African waters there were fewer dangers from the weather, except when the seas were stormy around the Cape of Good Hope. Poor defences and insufficient air cover made the task of the U-boats easier but the small number of German submarines meant that the Allied casualty rate was correspondingly reduced.

LONE WOLF ATTACKS

As early as 1941, the importance of the Cape route was appreciated by the Germans. All merchant ships travelling to and from Europe and Asia assembled at the port of Freetown in Sierra Leone and they then passed along the Cape of Good Hope. Ships taking that route stopped at a South African port in the course of their journey.

On arrival at Freetown faster vessels made their own way onwards, while slower ships formed themselves into convoys. This was seen by the Germans as an opportunity to pick off the lightly defended vessels, particularly as there was limited air cover for ships travelling that route. There were individual examples of German submarines attacking in South African waters before being there was part of the official strategy. For example, October and November 1941 saw *U-68* sink two ships off the coast of South-West Africa (now Namibia). Such lone wolf attacks were purely opportunist and until the decision to switch from the Atlantic to the less well protected African waters they were not only rare but were generally discouraged by the German navy.

OPERATION EISBÄR

Operation Eisbär, launched in October 1942, was the first deliberate U-boat campaign in South African waters. The lack of adequate defensive facilities or air cover made it highly successful and the complacency of British naval intelligence also assisted the submariners. The British believed that any U-boat campaign in South African waters would be limited and that the vast distances German submarines needed to travel to reach the Cape would make such attacks rare. They knew that German ships and a small force of U-boats operating in the South Atlantic might be capable of travelling to South Africa and launching sporadic attacks on shipping, but their main fear was that the Germans might mine the South African coast. In their opinion the greatest naval threat to South Africa came from Japanese submarines operating in Mozambique and the danger of a U-boat campaign was regarded as negligible.

The South Africans took the threat of German U-boats equally lightly. They believed that the most serious threat was posed by

Italian submarines operating from their bases in Ethiopia and Somalia, which were within range of South African targets. The defeat of the Italian forces in East Africa robbed the Axis of those bases and removed the danger of possible submarine attacks from Italy, but in spite of that neither the South Africans nor the British fully anticipated the swift transference of German U-boats to African waters.

The entry of Japan into the war led to a naval arrangement between the Germans and the Japanese over areas of submarine operation. By June 1942 Japanese submarines were active off the coast of Mozambique and in the course of a month they had sunk 19 merchant ships with the loss of over 86,000 tons. The British merchantman *Mundra* was lost less than 100 miles (160 km) from Durban.

This unexpected onslaught by the Japanese panicked the South Africans, who considered even a full-scale invasion of their country a possibility. It also forced the British to stretch their limited naval resources even more thinly by compelling them to defend a larger area of Asian waters in addition to their Atlantic and Arctic commitments. On the South African side, it led to a preoccupation with possible attacks on their eastern coast and a consequent neglect of the western side of their waters.

Only three South African ports possessed effective anti-submarine defences and the majority lacked protection by the South African Air Force. However, there was still complacency on the part of both the British and the South Africans about the possibility of German U-boat attacks. The first group of Eisbär U-boats sailed from Lorient in France on 20 August, with another German submarine leaving Bordeaux on the same date. They traversed 6,000 miles (9,600 km) before arriving in the waters off Cape Town.

There was disagreement between Dönitz and Raeder over the progress of the U-boats before they reached their destination. Dönitz believed their goal should be to maximize shipping losses and thought this could be achieved only through sinking vessels. Raeder, on the other hand, argued that the element of surprise was paramount and that the strategic goal of the mission – drawing off Allied ships from other routes – was of primary importance.

A compromise was eventually reached, but no successful attacks on convoys were made. The sinking of the *Laconia* was the only notable U-boat success during their progress towards South Africa. In the first week of October 1942 the wolfpack finally arrived off the coast of Cape Town.

On 8 October the attack began and caught the South African authorities completely by surprise. As German radio messages had not been intercepted the result was that the U-boats were able to destroy ships with impunity and within three days 14 vessels had been sunk.

The South Africans belatedly put security and defensive measures in place but Operation Eisbär had been a resounding success. More boats arrived to relieve the original pack with only a single U-boat being lost during this campaign. By December eight U-boats had sunk 53 merchant ships for the loss of a single submarine. Over 300,000 tons of shipping had been destroyed in the course of three months.[1]

SINKING OF THE *CITY OF CAIRO*

The second wave of U-boats in South African waters came in 1943 with the launch of Operation Seehund, when four submarines left the Bay of Biscay and were later reinforced by two more. The campaign was unsuccessful, however, as only 14 merchant ships were sunk for a total tonnage of 85,456. This failure was largely due to the defensive measures put in place by the South African authorities and the greater provision of air cover. No U-boats were lost, but Seehund had failed to inflict significant damage on merchant shipping. After that, most boats were recalled and by April 1943 only a single U-boat remained in South African waters. Nevertheless, it managed to sink three merchant ships. By mid-April, a second boat joined it, which only succeeded in sinking a single ship.

May proved more fruitful when four further U-boats arrived and the pack sank seven merchant ships. This was largely because the new boats were the improved Type IX, which could carry more fuel than the older U-boats, were faster and had greater range. Between May and August 26 merchant ships were sunk and nearly 150,000 tons of shipping were lost and, by the end of 1943, 50 merchantmen had been destroyed for a total of just under 300,000 tons, while the Germans had lost a single U-boat.

In December 1943 the *City of Cairo* was sunk. One of the survivors, Mrs Dulcie Kup, gave a vivid account of the tragedy:

> *About 8.30 p.m. [on 6 November] we felt a terrific thud and were nearly thrown off our chairs, all the lights immediately went out and I heard someone say 'We've got it this time'. Of course we couldn't see a thing, but I managed to grab my lifebelt from the back of my chair. I then dashed down the corridor as fast as I could to get Colin [her son] from the cabin. One flight of steps leading up the next deck and the boats had been completely blown away but we found the others intact. By the time we got up there my lifeboat was pretty full and no more men were allowed in. We were then lowered. We were*

not far off when the second torpedo struck. There was a terrific explosion, an enormous flame rose from the middle of the ship and spread outwards and then she completely disappeared. There was little noise, the sea was calm and we could see a little in the moonlight. Wreckage was everywhere.

As one of the lifeboats was being lowered the second torpedo was fired and everyone in it was thrown into the sea. All remaining boats rushed to their aid and space was eventually found for them. We already had 56 in our boat – 8 women. Colin was the only child. Our boat was designed to hold 48 people, so we were pretty cramped and really could take no more. We drifted about bumping into wreckage etc. It was then I began to wonder what would happen to us and I and some others were violently sick.

Kup described the rations issued to the people on the lifeboat – one biscuit, a Horlicks tablet and two ounces of water in the morning and the same rations in the evening, with the substitution of a small piece of chocolate for the Horlicks. They were in the lifeboat for 13 days during which she saw a man in another lifeboat fall overboard and drown. The weather was stormy much of the time and the journey was dangerous and stressful. She describes how:

By day it was very hot, but at night bitterly cold. Most of the time we had very high seas. How our little boat stuck together is a miracle. Sleep for me was not easy, sitting upright on narrow wooden seats with almost no back support. And so just as I was beginning to wonder whether it would not be best for Colin and me to slip over the side, things were looking so grim and we thought we had missed the island of St. Helena, a cargo ship loomed up on the horizon. It was about 4.30 a.m. on the thirteenth morning. It was pretty dark, the sun was just emerging. We couldn't believe our eyes at first. We had thought so often we had seen land or a ship in the distance but as she slowly came nearer we saw it really was true.

She goes on to relate the fate of the other lifeboats from the *City of Cairo.*

Boat No. 8 with fifty-five people on board had a defective mast and had been unable to keep up with any of the other boats. Early on their 14th morning and when morale was very low a ship was sighted. She came alongside and picked up the forty-seven Europeans and Asians who had survived and took them to Cape Town.

Tragically Boat No. 1 with twenty-three Europeans and thirty-one Asians sailed on for thirty-six days without sighting land or ship. At the end of the third week only eight people were still alive, but when the German freighter RHAKITIS found them only two British men and one woman were in the boat. Diana Jarman, a war widow 21 years old, had a very bad throat condition and the German doctor, having obtained permission from the two British men, decided he had to operate. Sadly she died under the anaesthetic. The two British men eventually reached home safely.

Boat No. 4 had an even more gruelling experience. It was a small boat holding only five British men, one

Australian woman, whose husband had been unable
to escape from the Cairo, and ten Asians. This boat
sailed on for fifty-one days and by then only Margaret
Gordon and James Knocker Whyte, Third Officer
of the Cairo, had survived the ordeal. They were
rescued by a Corvette of the Brazilian Navy when
they were only eight miles from the South American
coast having sailed over two thousand miles on their
own since 13th November. By then it was December
27th 1943.[2]

By the end of the year Dönitz came to regard the campaign in African waters as of little significance. The strength of the fleet was reduced and though there were isolated successes the cover by the South African Air Force and the RAF, coupled with more effective defensive measures, made it increasingly dangerous for U-boats to patrol that area. During 1944 eight merchant ships were sunk and 42,000 tons of shipping were lost, but in February 1945 a single merchant vessel was sunk. Effectively, the U-boat campaign in African waters had ceased to be a sustained attack by wolfpacks after August 1943 and had become a skirmishing expedition in the hope of catching unwary ships.

The total number of merchant ships sunk during the South African campaign was 114, with the loss of just under 700,000 tons of shipping. South African losses represented less than 5 per cent of the merchant tonnage destroyed by U-boats during the course of the Second World War.[3]

THE INGLORIOUS CAREER OF *U-1059*

The saga of *U-1059* is almost comical. Its captain, Günther Leupold, was only 23 years old and had never previously commanded a U-boat. When *U-1059* departed from Kiel on

Friday 4 February 1944 the crew considered this a bad omen as U-boats rarely sailed on a Friday. However, Leupold dismissed this fear as superstition and insisted that they sail on that date.

The submarine's mission was to avoid encounters with the enemy and make for its destination of Penang on the Malayan peninsula. From there it was supposed to attack Allied shipping before returning to France, but two days into the U-boat's journey Leupold discovered that its gun was damaged. After five days the gun was repaired and the boat sailed to the Arctic, past Iceland and the Faroe Islands, surfacing at night and submerging by day.

In late February the U-boat saw three fast freighters sailing to the west of Ireland. The captain had been ordered not to pursue them but he disregarded his instructions and set off after them. A futile chase made him realize he could not catch the ships and so he reluctantly resumed his intended course. The only result of this encounter was to deplete the boat's fuel to such an extent that he could not reach Penang without refuelling. On radioing his command base he was ordered to rendezvous with another submarine near the Cape Verde Islands on 25 March.

While sailing past the Azores *U-1059*'s captain discovered that all three of the boat's air compressors had failed, so he was compelled to remain on the surface for four days while they were repaired. At this point in the voyage Leupold's behaviour became markedly eccentric. As a result of travelling continually on the surface his boat was ahead of its scheduled rendezvous date and so he passed the time by allowing his crew to sunbathe, play chess, organize a concert and even swim in the warm waters, thus making them vulnerable to attack.

On 19 March 1944 Leupold and 17 crew members were swimming and most of the crew on board were either sleeping or playing cards. With the crew oblivious to approaching danger, the boat was an easy target for an aircraft carrier flying patrols in the vicinity. The planes spotted the U-boat with its 18 swimmers busy in the water and began attacking it with depth charges and machine-gun fire.

Those on the U-boat were startled and unprepared but fought back. Leupold raised the alarm and the boat's anti-aircraft guns began firing, but the depth charges broke the submarine in two and only 15 men survived. One of the two aircraft was hit by the flak from the U-boat and stalled before crashing into the water, only one of its crew surviving. Several of the U-boat survivors were wounded, including the captain, and out of the 15 submariners who had not been killed in the attack only eight were still alive when a rescue ship found them. That was the inglorious end of the brief career of *U-1059*. The survivors were unanimous in blaming their young and reckless captain for the failure of their mission.[4]

DRIVEN AWAY

U-66 made eight raids in the Atlantic before the boat was hit and its commander wounded. A new captain was then appointed and ordered to attack shipping off the coast of Africa. *U-66* left Lorient on 16 January 1944 and by the middle of February the boat had reached Freetown. At that point it prepared to attack a convoy but was driven away by a destroyer and air cover. Carrying on the search, on 26 February it located a convoy off the coast of Nigeria containing ten escorted merchant ships. The captain fired four torpedoes and hit a merchant ship, which began sinking. *U-66* was then subjected to hours of counter-attack by depth charges but though the electrics were damaged it managed to survive and escape.

On 1 March the U-boat was off the coast of Ghana when it attacked and sank a steamer travelling on its own. Then a few days later, on 5 March, the crew discovered another lone steamer off the Nigerian coast and sank that too. All of the crew survived and two were taken prisoner by the U-boat.

The next target was a tanker, which was attacked and sunk off the Nigerian coast on 21 March. At that point the boat's fuel supply began to run low and the captain requested a rendezvous for refuelling. This was arranged for late April off the Cape Verde Islands.

On 1 May, *U-66* found itself under constant surveillance from Allied aircraft, waiting for a chance to strike. Its designated refuelling boat had been sunk so another one was ordered to share its fuel reserves with the U-boat. Finding itself under attack from aircraft, *U-66* fired back and tried to escape but the escort ship *Buckley* pursued it and began firing at the U-boat. *U-66* was hit and began sinking before exploding. Thirty-six survivors were taken prisoner and 24, including the two British prisoners of war, died. The result of this episode was to convince Dönitz that it was impossible to continue refuelling his U-boats at sea as Allied superiority in the air and on the ocean made it too dangerous. He reluctantly issued a new order to his crews, declaring:

> All boats have received instructions to commence return passage in good time so that they can reach port without refuelling.[5]

Not only was this a humiliating admission of defeat but it restricted the range within which U-boats could operate, marking the beginning of the end for the U-boat menace.

ASIA

The entry of Japan into the war gave Germany both an ally and a new area of operations for its U-boats. What became known as the *Monsun Gruppe* (Monsoon Group), a group of U-boats that patrolled the Indian and Pacific Oceans, was established in 1942 and it then began to liaise with the Japanese, who also had submarines operating in the area. Until the country's surrender in 1943 Italian submarines also operated in the Pacific Ocean.

The main players in Asia were the Japanese and American navies. U-boats played a small and not very effective role in Pacific waters and most were lost during the conflict.

U-511 was the first German submarine to arrive in the Pacific. It carried the Japanese naval attaché from Berlin to Kure and the boat was presented to Japan, becoming *RO-500* in the Japanese submarine fleet. Its German crew then went to Penang where they established a submarine base, with a second one soon following at Kobe. Singapore, Jakarta and Surabaya then became the sites of U-boat repair bases. In early 1943, the captain of *U-178* sailed from South Africa to assume command of the base at Penang.[6]

The record of the Italian submarines destined for Asia was poor. One was sunk after aircraft bombed it in the Bay of Biscay in May 1943 and in June a second Italian submarine was bombed and destroyed by aircraft in the same area. The submarine *Comandante Cappellini* was more fortunate and managed to reach Singapore successfully in July 1943, transporting guns, ammunitions, bombsights, bomb prototypes, tank blueprints and aluminium, mercury and steel. *Giuliani* then managed to reach Singapore in August 1943 and *Torelli* reached Penang later the same month. Ironically it was not long before the Italian government made peace with the Allies and ordered its submarines to surrender. Those already in the Malaysian region were taken over by the Germans and given U-boat numberings.[7]

Before the base at Penang was fully operational *U-511* sank a Liberty ship on the way to its destination in July and *U-178* sank six ships before reaching Penang in late August. Of the eleven U-boats originally intended to be based there six were sunk before they reached their destination and the only Italian submarine en route surrendered when Italy made peace with the Allies. Four replacement boats were sent out but only one survived attack by Allied aircraft.

The fierce bombardment from the air continued to be a problem in transporting sufficient U-boats to Penang, as did warships and Allied submarines. In 1944 out of 23 U-boats sent on the trip only nine successfully reached Penang. The others were sunk by planes, torpedoed or depth charged. At the same time, 24 Allied vessels were sunk by the U-boats.

Penang was intended as a base from which U-boat patrols could be conducted to attack merchant ships and transport raw materials and supplies to Europe, but as the South Atlantic became too dangerous that plan was increasingly unsustainable. *U-178* carried a cargo of rubber, tungsten and tin and sank an American Liberty ship before successfully reaching France, while *U-532* carried a cargo of tungsten, tin, rubber, opium and quinine which was also intended for France. However, although *U-532* managed to sink a Liberty ship it was forced to return to Penang.

U-188 carried a similar cargo of opium, quinine, tungsten and tin and sank seven British ships before successfully reaching France, while *U-168* sank two ships before being forced to return to Jakarta. Another boat, *U-183*, failed to reach France and had to return to Penang on two occasions but sank three ships on the first voyage and one ship on the second.

The story was repeated over and over again, with limited success in sinking Allied ships and little success in transporting supplies to Europe. *U-1062* sailed from Penang bound for France but was sunk in the Atlantic and the former Italian submarine *Giuliani* was torpedoed by a Royal Navy warship. Only one successful U-boat patrol was carried out in the Pacific, which began in November 1944 and ended in February 1945, with two ships being sunk.[8]

The Pacific campaign was an unnecessary diversion of scarce resources and a costly failure. Individual successes were obtained, but the Allies' total superiority by both air and sea made the task of U-boats operating in the Pacific almost impossible. Deploying more of them in the Atlantic would have been a more productive use of their capabilities.

AUSTRALIA AND NEW ZEALAND

Twenty-eight Japanese and German submarines operated in the waters of Australia and New Zealand between 1942 and 1945. They sank 30 ships and killed over 600 people. The Royal Australian Air Force lost 23 planes during anti-submarine patrols off the coast whereas only one Japanese submarine was sunk and no U-boats were lost. Though this was a minor campaign, its effect was out of proportion to the numbers involved.[9]

In May 1944 a U-boat captain from the Monsoon Group recommended that Australia should be considered as a possible target. He believed that the element of surprise would mean a high probability of success.

The Japanese continually requested greater co-operation with the Germans in the Pacific and three submarines were sent to Australian waters. But their journeys required considerable preparation and spare parts and even torpedoes were difficult to obtain at such a distance. The Germans were also handicapped by a lack of information whereas the Australians received daily intelligence reports from Allied sources.

The first submarine to set sail was *U-168*, which left Djakarta on 5 October 1944. It was instructed to operate off the south-west coast of Australia. However, its signals were detected by the Allies and a submarine was despatched to intercept it.

On 6 October the Allied submarine saw and attacked *U-168*, firing six torpedoes. Two of them hit the boat and it sank with the loss of 23 crew members. Five survivors were rescued and taken for interrogation and others found sanctuary on a fishing vessel and made their way towards Japanese territory.

Meanwhile the victorious Allied submarine, *Zwaardvisch*, also sank four enemy ships before its return to Fremantle. On hearing of the loss of *U-168*, the Germans ordered *U-196* to make its way to Australia as a replacement.

U-537 was the next submarine to depart, leaving Surabaya on 9 November, but again the Allied superiority in intelligence-gathering doomed the U-boat. On 6 November three United States submarines were organized into a patrol and on 10 November they submerged and waited for their prey to arrive. The patrol report of one of the US boats, the *Flounder*, describes how an 'officer of the deck sighted what appeared to be a small sailboat' which was rapidly 'identified as a German submarine'. Four torpedoes were fired and the U-boat was hit inside the bow. It exploded and sank within 20 seconds, with none of the crew surviving.

The next U-boat to try its luck was *U-862*. After being refitted in Singapore it then sailed to Djakarta, before voyaging towards Australia on 18 November. *U-862* reached Cape Leeuwin on 28 November and searched for possible targets without success. After a week the captain decided that the Australian authorities must have warned shipping of the presence of a U-boat and so he steered it away from the normal routes.

On 9 December the submarine attempted to attack a Greek steamship off Cape Jaffa to the south of Adelaide, but the ship fired back and the U-boat decided to abort the attack. This led to the immediate despatch of two Australian corvettes to the area but they missed the U-boat. Its hydrophones had detected their presence so the boat had taken evasive action. South of Tasmania the boat encountered a tanker heading for New Zealand. *U-862* prepared to attack but when an aircraft was seen above it submerged and moved away.

Then on Christmas Eve *U-862* encountered an American Liberty ship. The submarine attacked for over three hours and it took five torpedoes before the ship sank. Royal Australian Air Force planes arrived after the ship had sunk and spent a fortnight searching for the U-boat, with warships also joining in the hunt. It turned out to be the longest and most extensive submarine search ever undertaken in Australian waters, but in spite of the Australian forces' perseverance they failed to detect the U-boat.

On 6 February 1945, the merchant ship *Peter Silvester* was travelling south-west of Australia when *U-862* fired two torpedoes which struck the starboard side of the vessel. One passed through the ship, but the other torpedo exploded in the hold. The ship began to flood and while attempting to right itself it was hit by two more torpedoes, again on the starboard side. The crew abandoned the vessel, which was then hit by a further torpedo and broke in half. Fifteen survivors took to a lifeboat and were rescued two days later, while a further 12 in another lifeboat and 80 on rafts were rescued the following day. It was not until 9 March that the final 15 crew members were picked up and landed safely. Thirty-three crew members died as a result of the sinking, which was the last successful U-boat attack in the Indian Ocean.[10]

In January 1945, *U-862* sailed along the east coast of New Zealand and tried but failed to attack a merchant ship off the coast of Napier. Two further unsuccessful attacks followed.

Soon afterwards the boat was ordered to return to Batavia. Its one and only mission in New Zealand waters had been a resounding failure.[11]

U-196 was the last U-boat sent to attack Australia. It left Djakarta on 30 November and was last seen heading towards south-west Australia. By the end of December nothing had been heard from the boat and though no Allied ship, submarine or plane claimed to have sunk the U-boat it had disappeared completely. The likelihood is that it struck an anti-submarine mine placed in Sunda Strait.[12]

NOTES

1 L.C.F. Turner, H.R. Gordon-Cumming and J. Betzler, *War in the Southern Oceans 1939–1945*, Oxford University Press, 1961

2 Account by Mrs Dulcie Kup of the sinking of the *City of Cairo*, in the Imperial War Museum archives

3 Evert Kleynhans, '"Good Hunting": German Submarine Offensives and South African Countermeasures off the South African Coast during the Second World War, 1942–1945', *Scientia Militaria*, vol. 44, no. 1, 2016

4 Paul Kemp, *U-boats Destroyed: German Submarine Losses in the World Wars*, Arms and Armour Press, 1997

5 BdU order, cited in Robert C. Stern, *Battle Beneath the Waves: The U-boat War*, Arms and Armour, 1999

6 Lawrence Paterson, *Hitler's Grey Wolves: U-boats in the Indian Ocean*, Greenhill, 2006

7 Ibid.

8 David Stevens, *U-boat Far from Home*, Allen and Unwin, 1997

9 Ibid.

10 Ibid.

11 Gerald Shone, *U-boat in New Zealand Waters*, Pahiatua Publications, 2016

12 Stevens, op. cit.

CHAPTER NINE
FINAL DEFEAT

The failure of the U-boat campaign was obvious by May 1943 but it was two more years before defeat was officially recognized. After Hitler and Goebbels committed suicide, Dönitz briefly succeeded as leader of Germany. By now Germany's surface ships had been destroyed, damaged or confined to harbours and the only operational part of the navy was the flotilla of U-boats. On 1 May 62 U-boats were still at sea.

Dönitz initially had no idea how Hitler had died but reluctantly accepted his role. He knew he could only delay inevitable defeat, but to buy time he made a belligerent radio broadcast in which he announced that the war would continue. He stated that:

> It is my first task to save Germany from destruction by the advancing Bolshevist enemy. For this aim alone the military struggle continues. As far and for so long as achievement of this aim is impeded by the British and the Americans we shall be forced to carry on our defensive fight against them as well.[1]

Dönitz did not make this speech purely for public consumption. He genuinely wanted to fight on, not in any expectation of victory, but to evacuate as many Germans as possible from the East in the face of the advancing Soviet troops. He knew the Russians had committed atrocities and though he would be the first to admit that Germany was hardly in a position to take the moral high ground on the issue of war crimes, he genuinely sought to protect those of his people that could be saved.

There were two main reasons why, even at this late stage, most Germans continued to resist rather than abandon a hopeless struggle. One was fear of the advancing Soviet forces but the other was an American government proposal for the treatment of Germany following an Allied victory.

US PLANS FOR GERMANY

The Treasury Secretary, Henry Morgenthau, had proposed a plan that involved reducing Germany to a pre-industrial level. It was originally the brainchild of Harry Dexter White, one of the senior Treasury officials and a man who had passed numerous military secrets to the Soviet Union. He was later investigated for spying but no charges were brought through lack of sufficient evidence to secure a conviction.

The post-war Germany envisaged by White was 'a country primarily agricultural and pastoral in its character'. He proposed that Germany should be completely demilitarized and have its industries closed down and relocated to other countries. Morgenthau became a strong champion of White's proposal and it soon became known as 'the Morgenthau Plan'.

In spite of opposition by senior members of his Cabinet, including his Secretary of State and his Secretary of War, Roosevelt was persuaded to adopt the plan and at the Quebec Conference in September 1944 it was signed by him and Churchill. Initially Churchill was reluctant to approve such a drastic treatment of the enemy but he was cajoled into signing by Roosevelt.

White gave a copy of the plan to Soviet intelligence and another member of the Treasury Department leaked it to the press. The result was a wave of public protests, after which

Roosevelt was forced to issue a public denial that the plan meant what it said. However, Goebbels then attempted to use the Morgenthau Plan as a means of motivating the Germans to fight on and he appears to have been successful. General Omar Bradley commented that after the release of the plan he had noticed 'a near-miraculous revitalization of the German army' and there is no doubt that it stiffened resolve and probably prolonged the war longer than necessary.[2]

DÖNITZ ABANDONS THE STRUGGLE

At the time Dönitz made his radio broadcast five U-boats were still operating around Canada and America and another submarine was sailing to the Caribbean. Only days remained before surrender but the U-boat crews showed no desire to abandon the fight. Seven were lost during combat over the next few days.

On 2 May, Dönitz commanded all U-boats stationed in Germany to make their way to Norway. He still clung on to the hope that somehow part of his flotilla could be saved. But the Allies sent aircraft to attack them and 21 submarines were lost. It then became obvious to Dönitz that there was no purpose in continuing.

On 4 May, he gave instructions to all U-boat crews to cease attacking Allied ships. They had not yet been commanded to surrender but it was not long before Dönitz issued that formal order. On the same day *U-853* sighted an American steamship and fired a torpedo. As the boat was submerged it had not received its new instructions. The steamship sank and 50 of the crew died. It was the last American ship to be sunk by a U-boat.

The U-boat training bases were abandoned as the Russians overran the Baltic ports where training had been conducted. In a final show of defiance Dönitz launched Operation Regenbogen (Operation Rainbow) in which he commanded the scuttling of the entire German fleet, both surface vessels and his flotilla of U-boats.

Once he had decided to abandon the struggle Dönitz began peace negotiations and sent an emissary to Montgomery to arrange the German surrender. He was determined to hold on in the East until the last minute and then surrender his forces to the Western Allies first. Montgomery told Dönitz's representative that he would accept surrender in Germany, Holland and Denmark but that the navy had to be turned over intact to the Allies. Dönitz was reluctant to comply with the British terms but realized that agreeing to them gave him more time to evacuate Germans from the East, before the advancing Soviet forces arrived. He decided, therefore, that it was better to accept the humiliation of turning over the fleet than to hinder the evacuation of troops and civilians, so on 4 May he contacted his navy, including his flotilla of U-boats, and ordered an immediate ceasefire.[3]

U-BOATS SURRENDER

The formal order to surrender did not come for another three days, as Dönitz was engaged in negotiations with the Americans, which were less successful than his meeting with the British. Eisenhower refused to meet the German envoy and insisted on unconditional surrender to all the Allied forces, including the Soviet Union. Dönitz had no choice but to agree, but was given 48 hours to complete the surrender.

U-boats were ordered to indicate they had surrendered by displaying a black flag and were required to keep their navigation lights turned on at night. On 8 May Admiral H.M. Burroughs of the Royal Navy transmitted orders for all U-boats to surface and fly a black flag and then report to the nearest Allied port. They were instructed to neutralize any torpedoes or mines, remove their guns and jettison their ammunition. All messages had to be transmitted in plain text and any refusal to comply would be treated as a hostile act.[4]

U-534 was one of the last U-boats to be sunk in action. On 4 May it was attempting to reach Norway when it was detected by Allied aircraft. The boat sank a Liberator but was depth-charged by the second plane and 52 survivors were picked up by lifeboats.

Rumours began to circulate that it was carrying gold bullion and looted artwork and high-ranking Nazis were among the crew. However, in 1993 a salvage team examined the wreck and discovered nothing of value on board. Its cargo was normal U-boat fare and the only materials found were tinned food and condoms. The boat was acquired by the Warship Preservation Trust and is on display at the Nautilus Maritime Museum in Birkenhead.[5]

U-979 was one of the last German submarines to sink Allied shipping. On 2 May, it accounted for a British trawler west of Reykjavík and on 5 May it sank a British tanker. Only then did the crew learn of Dönitz's order, as their radio had been out of action. The captain decided not to surrender to the Icelandic authorities but instead sailed back to Germany. On 23 May the boat arrived at the North Friesian islands, where it was deliberately wrecked. Although the boat's commander was arrested for breaking the ceasefire, he was able to prove that he had not received the message until the day after his attack on the tanker.[6]

On 7 May, the last offensive actions were undertaken by U-boats, when three ships were sunk off the coast of France. These attacks contravened Dönitz's ceasefire order issued to all U-boats on 4 May, though his formal capitulation was not received by some until 9 May. The sinkings were a last act of defiance before the end of the war in Europe.

In spite of their new instructions to surrender, many U-boat captains decided to follow their previous orders to scuttle under Operation Regenbogen. As a result, 217 U-boats were scuttled before the countermanding order was received and a further 16 boats that were not operational were also destroyed. The remaining U-boats then surrendered over the next few weeks.

The first U-boats to surrender were *U-143*, *U-145*, *U-149*, *U-150*, *U-368*, *U-720* and *U-1230*, all of which surrendered to the Allies at Heligoland. On the same day *U-155*, *U-680* and *U-1233* surrendered at Baring Bay, near Frederica in Denmark and *U-291*, *U-779*, *U-883*, *U-1103*, *U-1406*, *U-1407*, *U-2341* and *U-2356* surrendered at Cuxhaven in Germany.[7]

Other vessels followed over the next few days. *U-249* raised its black flag off the Scilly Isles on 8 May and two Royal Navy vessels escorted it to Portland Bight. Another followed quickly and surrendered to a British minesweeper in the Outer Hebrides.[8]

By 19 May, all but two of the U-boats had surrendered either to Allied forces or to neutral countries. Only two refused to give themselves up and as a result they became the source of many myths and fantasies. The captains of *U-530* and *U-977* refused to surrender and offered the crew a choice of being disembarked or of trying to escape to a safe neutral country. Some chose to leave the boats and take refuge in Norway but most decided to try to evade pursuit.

On 10 July, *U-530* arrived at Mar del Plata in Argentina and surrendered to the Argentine authorities. After an even longer voyage *U-977* also reached Mar del Plata and turned itself over to the waiting officials.

The epic voyages of both U-boats have become the stuff of conspiracy theories. The truth is more prosaic. A combination of outstanding seamanship by the captains of both vessels and

A German submarine crew bring their U-boat to an assembly point from which it was towed to the destruction point and destroyed by gunfire. British and Irish naval ships accompanied the U-boats to the destruction point 10 miles (16 km) west of Donegal, where Operation Deadlight was carried out.

perhaps lax security following the end of hostilities allowed them to travel for much of the time submerged. *U-977* in particular spent the majority of its journey to Argentina under the water and the crew were in poor physical shape when they finally surrendered.

In spite of all the fantasies that have been woven around these voyages, neither U-boat took Hitler, Bormann or Nazi treasures to a safe location in South America or elsewhere. Their journeys were remarkable but simply demonstrated the courage, resourcefulness and endurance of their crews.[9]

The surrender of *U-234* on 19 May remains controversial, though it is not disputed that scientific material was removed from the boat after American authorities took possession. *U-234* carried an unusual cargo and some high-ranking officers. Two were Japanese and they committed suicide rather than surrender to the Americans. The others were German with four officers from the navy, four from the Luftwaffe and two Messerschmitt engineers, whose area of expertise was jet and rocket engines.

U-234's cargo included a glide bomb, mercury, cameras, infrared fuses, anti-tank weapons, optical glass, blueprints, two disassembled Messerschmitt Me262 fighters and a quantity of uranium-235 oxide. Once it docked the U-boat was systematically looted but there remains controversy over the status and fate of the uranium on board.

The boxes containing uranium were opened and the contents removed. An American civilian observed the proceedings and the U-boat officer supervising the cargo's dispersal asked who he was. The laconic answer was 'Oppenheimer', which might well have been true as J. Robert Oppenheimer was a key US atomic physicist.

The US was short of enriched uranium and its scientists had failed to devise a way to trigger a plutonium bomb. According to Schlicke, one of the naval officers on board the U-boat and an expert on infrared technology, he was asked to assist the Americans. He then transported the fuses to Washington and helped them develop the plutonium bomb that was dropped on Nagasaki. *U-234*'s cargo of uranium would also have filled the American shortage of that material, which then allowed the US to drop a uranium bomb on Hiroshima. Nazi scientists were not far behind the West in developing atomic weapons and *U-234*'s cargo and Schlicke's expertise ushered in the atomic age.[10]

The majority of U-boat crews were unhappy about surrendering but had no choice. They would have been willing to fight on if necessary but many captains preferred to scuttle their boats rather than let them fall into Allied hands. Those U-boats still operating in Asia were commandeered by the Japanese and transferred to their navy. The German crews were then replaced by Japanese men and became prisoners of war.

One of the strangest aspects of the surrender was that 33 U-boats congregated in a Scottish loch for the process. Loch Eriboll in the Sutherland area was chosen for its deep anchorage and isolated position, a precautionary measure against any aggressive action by the crewmen. Between 10 and 25 May the surrender of the once feared ocean predators was concluded.[11]

One hundred and fifty-six U-boats surrendered to the Allies and a process of destruction began.[12] First of all, 116 boats were scuttled under what was codenamed Operation Deadlight, a Royal Navy operation. The original plan was to tow the U-boats to various areas to the north-west of Ireland and sink them. Some were destined to be scuttled and others were to be used as targets for bombers. The third group was sunk by ships either through explosive charges or naval guns.

Once the U-boats were in Allied hands it was discovered that many were in such bad condition that 56 of them sank before they could be towed to the areas designated for scuttling them. Explosive charges often failed to sink the U-boats and it was necessary to resort to gunfire to sink them. The first U-boat was sunk under Operation Deadlight on 17 November 1945 and the last one on 11 February 1946.[13] Not all U-boats came under the auspices of Operation Deadlight. Four were still in Asia when the Germans surrendered and the Japanese quickly commandeered them.

Forty-nine U-boats were not destroyed. Seven were sunk in Asia, two in the US, four were scrapped in Norway and one became part of the French navy. Ten were then handed over to the Russians, ten to the Americans, ten to the British, one to the Dutch and four to Norway. One of the British boats was transferred to Canada and two more went to the French. Of the seven U-boats which had been taken over by the Japanese following the German surrender, all were either scuttled or sunk.

Only two wartime U-boats now survive – *U-505* which was saved by American Rear Admiral Daniel V. Gallery, who claimed it as a prize of war and ensured that it was transferred to the Museum of Science and Industry in Chicago, and *U-995*, which the Norwegians handed over to Britain in October 1948. *U-995* was later returned to Germany in 1965 and is now in a museum.[14]

During the final stages of the war U-boat crew members based in Hamburg, Kiel and Wilhelmshaven found themselves disembarked and enrolled into the infantry. They began using rifles and bazookas rather than torpedoes and deck guns.

In spite of their inexperience the U-boat men fought as fiercely on land as at sea. The men of the 2nd Naval Division distinguished themselves at the Battle of Rethem when British troops attacked on 11 April. They were driven back with heavy casualties and reinforcements had to be summoned. Even their enemies paid tribute to their bravery:

*They were nearly all ex-sailors, many of them until
lately members of submarine crews. They had had
little time for military training and therefore lacked
the fighting skills of the paratroopers, but their
discipline and bravery were exemplary.*[15]

It is ironic that some of the last fighting seen by U-boat crews
was on land, defending the harbours from which their boats had
once sailed out to be the terror of the oceans.

U-BOAT BASES DESTROYED

Not only the U-boats themselves but the bases and bunkers that
were built to accommodate and repair them were dismantled
or destroyed. At the end of the war a number of U-boat bases
and bunkers in foreign countries were still held by the Germans.
The most important were La Pallice (the deep-water harbour
of La Rochelle), Brest, Saint-Nazaire, Bordeaux and Lorient
in France. They had survived seven months under siege and
no longer functioned as operational bases. Among the forces
defending Lorient were 780 U-boat crew members.

The central defences of the main U-boat bases were concrete
bunkers constructed by the Todt Organization. Saint-Nazaire
had two defensive mortar positions, one a raised emplacement
at the rear containing an M19, two casements housing a Skoda
Pak36 and heavy machine guns. In addition, anti-tank obstacles
were placed to block overland routes to the base. Even the
British raid in 1942 failed to neutralize the base, though the
task force succeeded in blowing up the lock gates.

After a failed attempt to take it by storm Lorient was besieged
by Allied armies. It was protected by the natural barriers of the
Etel and Scorff rivers, land approaches were heavily mined and
anti-tank ditches protected the base. The three large U-boat

bunkers at Lorient, which were capable of accommodating 30 U-boats under cover, were actually built in 1941 at the neighbouring fishing port of Keroman. They were imposing and were nicknamed 'Dom Bunkers' because of their similarity to cathedral arches. Lorient, or Keroman, was the largest of the German bases in France and nearly 500 submarine missions were carried out from there. In spite of repeated bombing raids on Lorient the Keroman base survived and was still intact at the end of the war. The entire site was one vast concrete bunker and after a while people became inured to repeated air raids. French and Russian workers carried out many of the menial tasks on the base, but they frequently tried to sabotage the U-boats by putting sand in their engines. Ironically, U-boat crews were deeply unpopular with other branches of the German armed forces because they gave food and cigarettes to the Russian prisoners working as forced labour.

Attempts to destroy the base and its submarine pens failed and instead the Allies launched a massive raid on Lorient to cut off the supply chain for the U-boat base. It was impossible for the Keroman facility to receive fuel, provisions and torpedoes, which prevented the submarines at the base from aggressively patrolling the Atlantic. Keroman held out until the final surrender in the West and remained a German enclave in France long after the liberation of the bulk of the nation. It finally surrendered on 10 May, two days after the official end of the war in Europe.[16]

La Rochelle was covered with concrete and thick steel and consisted of ten cells. It was able to house 13 submarines and ten repair and storage yards. A new lock was built in 1942 to allow the U-boats to enter and exit and it was protected by a strong bunker. Anti-aircraft and anti-submarine devices were also fitted which made the base easily defensible, as the Allies discovered when trying to destroy it.[17]

Bombers of the US 8th Army Air Force pound the German U-boat base at Saint-Nazaire and cause massive damage, January 1944.

Bordeaux was originally shared with the Italian navy, but the Germans soon discovered that the size of the Italian submarine fleet was not matched by its efficiency. Over a two-month period in 1940 each Italian boat sank an average of 20 tonnes a day while the U-boats sank 1,115 tonnes. As bombing campaigns against the base began in September 1941, protective bunkers were built.[18]

Brest was heavily bombed but until Barnes Wallis's Tallboy bombs were used against it the structure was not seriously damaged.[19]

NOTES

1   Paterson, *Black Flag*
2   An attempt to defend the Morgenthau Plan was made by its main advocate. Henry Morgenthau, *Germany is Our Problem*, Harper & Brothers, 1945
3   Paterson, *Black Flag*
4   Ibid.
5   Robert C. Stern, *Battle Beneath the Waves*
6   Paterson, *Black Flag*
7   https://uboat.net/fates/surrendered.htm?display=date/
8   Paterson, *Black Flag*
9   Ibid.
10 Georg Högel, *U-boat Emblems of World War II 1939–1945*, Schiffer, 1999
11 David M. Hird, *The Grey Wolves of Eriboll*, Whittles Publishing, 2010
12 'Operation "Deadlight": Coastal Command Attack Surrendered U-Boats', *Flight*, 27 December 1945
13 Paterson, *Black Flag*
14 Ibid.
15 Earl of Rosse and E.R. Hill, *The Story of the Guards Armoured Division*, Geoffrey Bles, 1956
16 Jak P. Mallmann Showell, *Hitler's U-boat Bases*, Sutton Publishing, 2002
17 Ibid.
18 Ibid.
19 Ibid.

AFTERMATH

The casualty figures for merchant seamen and U-boat crews were horrific. Over 2,400 British merchant ships were sunk, with the loss of more than 30,000 lives and over 70 Canadian merchant ships were lost, at a cost of 1,600 seamen killed. The USA lost 733 merchant ships at a cost of 8,651 lives and 694 Norwegian vessels were lost and around 3,700 sailors died in action. On the German side, out of a total of 1,156 U-boats built 793 were lost and over 28,000 crew members were killed.

During the war U-boats sank nearly 3,000 ships and a total of over 14 million tons was lost. They accounted for 70 per cent of all shipping losses by the Allies during the war. The British lost 1,660 ships to the U-boats, the US 549, Norway 314, Holland 137 and Greece 124.

Fatalities among merchant seamen were higher than any branch of the armed services with 20 per cent being killed over the course of the war. In 1941 and 1942 this figure rose to a staggering 49 per cent. The same was true of U-boat crews, who suffered a casualty rate of 75 per cent.

ALLIED TREATMENT OF PRISONERS

The fate of U-boat crew members following Germany's surrender varied wildly. Those who were captured by the Russians found themselves despatched to the Gulags as forced labour and many died as a result. When Churchill remarked to Stalin at the Potsdam Conference that there was a shortage of labour for building work and coal mining, the Soviet dictator immediately suggested using German prisoners of war for the task. Churchill

Hitler's military thinking was influenced by his experiences during World War I and he perhaps never fully understood the crucial role a larger submarine fleet might have played in subduing Britain and her allies.

demurred and Stalin seemed surprised at his reluctance, claiming that there was 'more meat on the German bone', which could be used to fill any labour shortages.[1]

U-boat men, like other branches of the German armed forces, suffered from the arbitrary decision by Eisenhower to reclassify German POWs as 'disarmed enemy personnel' rather than surrendered combatants. This 'reclassification' enabled the Allies to ignore their rights as POWs under the Geneva Convention. Instead of being repatriated after a brief period in custody they found themselves being used as forced labour. Conditions in some camps were frequently poor, with Remagen being the most notorious, and hundreds of German prisoners died in these camps from starvation.[2]

On the whole, however, U-boat crews taken prisoner by the British and Americans fared better than this and though they might have been used as forced labour, they were not otherwise abused. The crew of *U-546* were an exception. After the boat was sunk, it was taken to Newfoundland and then the captain, eight officers and the specialist staff were separated from the rest of the crew and taken away by the Americans. After that, they were subjected to eight days of beatings. The captain's treatment was so brutal that a US officer protested when he observed it, which merely led to the German being moved to another prison. Eventually he wrote an account telling the American authorities about all of the equipment on board his submarine and the duties in which it had been engaged.[3]

The fate of Friedrich Steinhoff, captain of *U-873*, was even worse. On 7 May his boat detected the presence of warships on the hydrophone and then it received instructions to surrender. Steinhoff ordered it to surface and fly a suitable flag. The U-boat did not possess a black flag so a dark green curtain was hung on the periscope. An American destroyer approached and a boarding party entered *U-873*. On 17 May the U-boat was escorted to the naval base in New Hampshire. The crew were taken to cells and held in solitary confinement, while Steinhoff was singled out for brutal treatment, almost certainly because his brother Ernst was one of the leading rocket scientists at Peenemünde, where development and production of the V-2 rocket took place.

For two days Steinhoff was brutally beaten and other prisoners testified to hearing his screams. The U-boat doctor, also among the captives, insisted on seeing the prisoner. Reluctantly the guards unlocked his cell door, where he was found lying in a pool of blood.

Steinhoff was still alive, so the doctor demanded his immediate transfer to hospital. The doctor argued with the guards, who were deliberately obstructive, and it was two hours before an ambulance arrived. By that time Steinhoff was dead. Broken by his brutal treatment, he had slashed his wrists and bled to death.

An inquiry was held which revealed that U-boats had been systematically looted and the property of prisoners stolen. Individuals were found to have 'exceeded their authority' and were guilty of 'dereliction of duty', but they were not punished beyond being issued with 'letters of reprimand'. Effectively the inquiry whitewashed the people responsible for these actions and no proper punishment was administered.[4]

Those who became prisoners of the French were often treated harshly, being condemned to live outdoors without shelter and on only meagre rations. Some were offered their freedom if they joined the French Foreign Legion but those who enlisted were soon shipped off to fight the long and unsuccessful war in Vietnam.[5]

The restored Norwegian government compelled German prisoners of war to clear minefields. This task was not completed until September 1946 and in the course of the work 275 German POWs were killed and 392 injured. This was directly contrary to the Geneva Convention, which specifically states: 'It is forbidden to use prisoners of war on unhealthful or dangerous work.' The Norwegians used the 'reclassification' of POWs by Eisenhower as 'disarmed enemy forces' as their excuse for making them clear minefields.[6]

These instances of the maltreatment of German prisoners and the flagrant violation of the Geneva Convention at Eisenhower's instruction might have raised more protesting voices if the world had not become aware of the horrors of the concentration camps and of Nazi genocide.

In those circumstances it is hardly surprising that sympathy for Germans was in short supply. In addition to the revulsion caused by the revelations of brutality under the Third Reich a special fear and hatred was felt towards U-boat crews. This detestation was unjust, as they were no more to be reproached for the death toll they inflicted than pilots, sailors on warships or soldiers. Being sunk by a submarine was no more an attack by stealth than an aircraft dropping bombs on civilians.

However irrational this hatred was, it undoubtedly influenced the treatment of U-boat crews, who were consistently treated more harshly and held prisoner longer than other branches of the German military. This is doubly unjust as their casualties were proportionately higher than any other section of the armed forces.

FINAL SUMMARY
Naval battles like Trafalgar and Jutland are remembered but in the Second World War a long battle of attrition between

U-boats and merchantmen rather than a single encounter decided the outcome of the conflict and made victory possible. The sea became the anonymous graveyard of thousands and their courage and endurance deserve to be remembered.

NOTES

1   Churchill, *Second World War*
2   Paterson, *Black Flag*
3   Ibid.
4   Ibid.
5   Ibid.
6   Ibid.

BIBLIOGRAPHY

Patrick Abazzia, *Mr Roosevelt's Navy: The Private War of the US Atlantic Fleet,
1939–1942*, Naval Institute Press, 1975

R.J.Q. Adams, *British Politics and Foreign Policy in the Age of Appeasement*, Stanford
University Press, 1993

Field Marshal Lord Alanbrooke, *War Diaries, 1939–1945*, Phoenix, 2002

Jim Allaway, *Hero of the Upholder*, Periscope Publishing, 2004

Walter Ansel, *Hitler Confronts England*, Duke University Press, 1960

Anne Armstrong, *Unconditional Surrender: The impact of the Casablanca policy upon
World War II*, Rutgers University Press, 1961

Warren Armstrong, *Salt Water Tramps*, Jarrolds, 1945

Max Arthur, *Lost Voices of the Royal Navy*, Ebury, 2005

A.J. Barker, *Dunkirk: The Great Escape*, Dent, 1977

Corelli Barnett, *Engage the Enemy More Closely*, Hodder and Stoughton, 1991
— *Hitler's Generals*, Grove Weidenfeld, 1989

Paul Beaver, *U-boats in the Atlantic*, Patrick Stephens, 1979

Patrick Beesley, *Very Special Intelligence*, Hamish Hamilton, 1977

Antony Beevor, *The Battle for Spain: The Spanish Civil War 1936–1939*, Phoenix,
2006

Edward W. Bennett, *German Rearmament and the West, 1932–1933*, Princeton
University Press, 2015

G.H. Bennett and R. Bennett, *Survivors: British Merchant Seamen in the Second World
War*, Hambledon, 1999

Keith W. Bird, *Erich Raeder: Admiral of the Third Reich*, Naval Institute Press, 2006

Clay Blair, *Hitler's U-boat War*, Cassell, 2000

Martin Bowman, *Deep Sea Hunters: RAF Coastal Command and the War Against the
U-Boats and the German Navy 1939–1945*, Pen and Sword, 2014

Robin Brodhurst, *Churchill's Anchor: A Biography of Admiral of the Fleet Sir Dudley
Pound*, Pen and Sword, 2000

Captain Jack Broome, *The Convoy is to Scatter*, William Kimber, 1972

David K. Brown, *Atlantic Escorts: Ships, Weapons and Tactics in World War II*, Naval
Institute Press, 2007

Louis Brown, *A Radar History of World War II*, Institute of Physics Publishing, 1999

Robert Buderi, *The Invention that Changed the World: How a Small Group of Radar Pioneers Won the Second World War and Launched a Technical Revolution*, Touchstone, 1997

Thomas B. Buell, *Master of Seapower: A Biography of Fleet Admiral Ernest J. King*, Naval Institute Press, 2012

John Gorley Bunker, *Liberty Ships: The Ugly Ducklings of World War II*, Naval Institute Press, 1972

Harold Busch, *U-boats at War: German Submarines in Action, 1939–1945*, Ballantine, 1955

Ragnar Busch and Hans-Joachim Döll, *U-boat Commanders*, Greenhill, 1996

J.R.M. Butler, *History of the Second World War*, Grand Strategy, vol. II, HMSO, 1976

John Campbell, *Naval Weapons of World War Two*, Naval Institute Press, 1985

Alan C. Carey, *Galloping Ghosts of the Brazilian Coast*, iUniverse, 2004

F.L. Carsten, *The Reichswehr and Politics 1918 to 1933*, University of California, 1966

Max Caulfield, *A Night of Terror: The story of the* Athenia *affair*, Muller, 1958

W.S. Chalmers, *Max Horton and the Western Approaches: A Biography of Admiral Sir Max Kennedy Horton, GCB, DSO*, Hodder and Stoughton, 1954

Terry Charman, *Outbreak 1939: The World Goes to War*, Virgin, 2009

Winston S. Churchill, *The Second World War*, 6 vols, Cassell, 1948

Richard Compton-Hall, *The Underwater War 1939–1945*, Blandford, 1982

John Costello and Terry Hughes, *The Battle of the Atlantic*, Collins, 1977

Peter Cremer, *U-333: The Story of a U-boat Ace*, Triad Grafton, 1986

Admiral of the Fleet Viscount Cunningham, *A Sailor's Odyssey*, Hutchinson, 1951

Robert Dallek, *Franklin D. Roosevelt and American Foreign Policy, 1932–1945*, Oxford University Press, 1995

Kev Darling, *Fleet Air Arm Carrier War: The History of British Naval Aviation*, Pen and Sword, 2009

T.K. Derry and J.R.M. Butler, *The Campaign in Norway. History of the Second World War*, United Kingdom Military Series, HMSO, 1952

Jonathan Dimbleby, *The Battle of the Atlantic: How the Allies Won the War*, Viking, 2015

Robert Divine, *Roosevelt and World War II*, Johns Hopkins University Press, 1969

Karl Dönitz, *Ten Years and Twenty Days*, Weidenfeld & Nicolson, 1959

James Douglas-Hamilton, *The Air Battle for Malta*, Airlife, 1981

Cherry Drummond, *The Remarkable Life of Victoria Drummond – Marine Engineer*, Institute of Marine Engineers, 1994

Spencer Dunmore, *In Great Waters: The Epic Story of the Battle of the Atlantic*, McClelland and Stewart, 1999

David Dutton, *Neville Chamberlain*, Bloomsbury Academic, 2001

Bernard Edwards, *War of the U-boats: British Merchant Vessels Under Fire*, Pen and Sword, 2006

Edward E. Ericson, *Feeding the German Eagle: Soviet Economic Aid to Nazi Germany, 1933–1941*, Greenwood Publishing Group, 1999

Vincent J. Esposito (ed.), *A Concise History of World War II*, Praeger Publishers, 1964

Richard J. Evans, *The Third Reich in Power*, Penguin, 2005

Jonathan Fenby, *The Sinking of the 'Lancastria': Britain's greatest maritime disaster and Churchill's cover-up*, Simon and Schuster, 2005

Wolfgang Frank, *The Sea Wolves*, Ballantine, 1981

Norbert Frei, *National Socialist Rule in Germany: The Führer State, 1939–1945*, Blackwell, 1993

Willi Frischauer and Robert Jackson, *The Navy's Here! The Altmark Affair*, Victor Gollancz, 1955

Michael Gannon, *Operation Drumbeat*, Naval Institute Press, 1990

Robert Gardiner (ed.), *Conway's All the World's Fighting Ships, 1922–1946*, Mayflower Books, 1980

Robert Glenton, *The Royal Oak Affair: The Saga of Admiral Collard and Bandmaster Barnacle*, Leo Cooper, 1991

Jack Greene and Alessandro Massignani, *The Naval War in the Mediterranean, 1940–1943*, Chatham Publishing, 1998

Peter Gretton, *Convoy Escort Commander*, Cassell, 1964

Erich Gröner, *German Warships: 1815–1945*, Naval Institute Press, 1990

F. Grossmith, *The Sinking of the* Laconia, *A Tragedy in the Battle of the Atlantic*, Watkins Publishing, 1994

Geirr H. Haarr, *The Gathering Storm: The Naval War in Northern Europe September 1939–April 1940*, Seaforth Publishing, 2013

Arnold Hague, *The Allied Convoy System, 1939–1945: Its Organization, Defence and Operation*, Vanwell Publications, 2000

— *Sloops, 1926–1946*, World Ship Society, 1993

W.A. Haskell, *Shadows on the Horizon: The Battle of Convoy HX233*, Naval Institute Press, 1998

Albert P. Heiner, *Henry J. Kaiser: Western Colossus*, Halo, 1991

Waldo Heinrichs, *Threshold of War: Franklin D. Roosevelt and American Entry into WWII*, Oxford University Press, 1988

Arthur Herman, *Freedom's Forge: How American Business Produced Victory in World War II*, Random House, 2012

Günther Hessler, *The U-boat War in the Atlantic*, HMSO, 1989

Arthur Hezlet, *The Submarine and Sea Power*, Peter Davis, 1967

E.H. Hinsley and Alan Stripp, *Code Breakers: The Inside Story of Bletchley Park*, Oxford University Press, 2001

David M. Hird, *The Grey Wolves of Eriboll*, Whittles Publishing, 2010

Wolfgang Hirschfeld and Geoffrey Brooks, *Hirschfeld – The Story of a U-boat NCO 1940–46*, Leo Cooper, 1996

Georg Högel, *U-boat Emblems of World War II 1939–1945*, Schiffer, 1999

Fred Horman, *Dynamite Cargo: Convoy to Russia*, Vanguard, 1943

James Howard, *The War in the West, vol. 1, Germany Ascendant, 1939–1941*, Bantam, 2015
— *The War in the West, vol. 2, The Allies Fight Back, 1941–1943*, Bantam, 2017

Sir Archibald Hurd, *Britain's Merchant Navy*, Odhams, 1943

Robert Hutchinson, *Jane's Submarines: War Beneath the Waves from 1776 to the Present Day*, Harper Collins, 2001

David Irving, *The Destruction of PQ17*, Granada, 1985

Max Jacobson, *The Diplomacy of the Winter War: The Soviet Attack on Finland 1939–1940*, Harvard University Press, 1961

Geoffrey Jones, *Defeat of the Wolf Packs*, William Kimber, 1986

R.V. Jones, *Most Secret War: British Scientific Intelligence 1939–1945*, Hamish Hamilton, 1978

John Jordan and Stephen Dent (eds), *Warship 2013*, Conway, 2013

John Jordan and Robert Dumas, *French Battleships 1922–1956*, Seaforth Publishing, 2009

Philip Kaplan, *Grey Wolves: The U-boat War 1939–1945*, Pen & Sword, 2014

Robert Gordon Kaufman, *Arms Control During the Pre-Nuclear Era: The United States and Naval Limitation Between the Two World Wars*, Columbia University Press, 1990

John Keegan, *The Price of Admiralty*, Viking, 1989

Paul Kemp, *U-boats Destroyed – German Submarine Losses in the World Wars*, Arms and Armour, 1999

Paul M. Kennedy, *The Rise and Fall of British Naval Mastery*, Allen Lane, 1976

William King, *The Stick and the Stars*, Norton, 1958

F.H. Kinsley and Alan Stripp, *Codebreakers: The Inside Story of Bletchley Park*, Oxford University Press, 1993

Burton H. Klein, *Germany's Economic Preparations for War*, Harvard University Press, 1968

William L. Langer, S. Gleason, S. Everett, *The Undeclared War 1940–1941: The World Crisis and American Foreign Policy*, Harper, 1953

Bill Linskey, *No Longer Required*, Pisces Press, 1999

The Earl of Longford and Thomas P. O'Neill, *Éamon de Valera*, Arrow, 1974

Robert W. Love, *History of the US Navy, vol.1, 1775–1941*, Stackpole Books, 1992

Thomas P. Lowry and John W.G. Wellham, *The Attack on Taranto: Blueprint for Pearl Harbor*, Stackpole Books, 1995

Paul Lund and Harry Ludlam, *PQ17 – Convoy to Hell*, New English Library, 1969
— *Night of the U-boats*, Foulsham, 1973

John MacDonald, *Great Battles of World War II*, Strathearn Books, 1986

Donald McIntyre, *U-boat Killer*, Cassell, 1956
— *Narvik*, W.W. Norton, 1959

Joseph Maiolo, *The Royal Navy and Nazi Germany, 1933–39: A Study in Appeasement and the Origins of the Second World War*, Macmillan, 1998

Alistair Mars, *British Submarines at War 1939–1945*, William Kimber, 1971

David Mason, *U-boat: The Secret Menace*, Macdonald, 1968

Robert K. Massie, *Castles of Steel: Britain, Germany and the Winning of the Great War at Sea*, Ballantine Books, 2004

Keith Middlemas and John Barnes, *Baldwin*, Littlehampton Book Services, 1969

David Miller, *U-Boats: The Illustrated History of the Raiders of the Deep*, Brasseys, 2000

Morris O. Mills, *Convoy PQ13: Unlucky for Some*, Bernard Durnford, 2000

W.H. Mitchell and L.A. Sawyer, *The Empire Ships*, Lloyds of London Press, 1990

Henry Morgenthau, *Germany is Our Problem*, Harper & Brothers, 1945

Samuel Eliot Morison, *The Battle of the Atlantic: 1939–1945*, Little, Brown, 1947

Karl-August Muggenthaler, *German Raiders of World War II*, Robert Hale, 1978

Timothy P. Mulligan, *Neither Sharks Nor Wolves*, Chatham, 1999

Thomas Munch-Petersen, *The Strategy of Phoney War: Britain, Sweden and the Iron Ore Question 1939–1940*, Militärhistoriska studier, 1981

Axel Niestlé, *German U-Boat Losses During World War II*, Greenhill, 1998

Peter Padfield, *War Beneath the Sea: Submarine Conflict During World War II*, Wiley, 1998

— *Dönitz, The Last Führer: Portrait of a Nazi War Leader*, Thistle Publishing, 2013

Lawrence Paterson, *U-boats in the Mediterranean*, Chatham, 2006

— *Black Flag: The Surrender of Germany's U-boat Forces 1945*, Seaforth, 2009

— *Schnellboote: A Complete Operational History*, Seaforth Publishing, 2015

Kenneth Poolman, *Periscope Depth*, Sphere, 1984

Richard A. Preston, *The Defence of the Undefended Border: Planning for War in North America 1867–1939*, McGill-Queens University Press, 1977

Alfred Price, *Spitfire Mark I/II Aces 1939–41*, Osprey Publishing, 2012

Günther Prien, *Fortunes of War – U-boat Commander*, Tempus, 2000

Erich Raeder, *Struggle for the Sea*, William Kimber, 1959

David Reynolds, *The Creation of the Anglo-American Alliance, 1937–1941*, University of North Carolina Press, 1982

Stephen Roberts, *The House that Hitler Built*, Methuen, 1937

Terence Robertson, *Walker RN: Britain's Ace U-Boat Killer*, Pan, 1958

Jürgen Rohwer, *Axis Submarine Successes 1939–1945*, Patrick Stephens, 1982

Earl of Rosse and E.R. Hill, *The Story of the Guards Armoured Division*, Geoffrey Bles, 1956

Captain S.W. Roskill, *The War at Sea, 1939–1945, vol. 1, The Defensive*, HMSO, 1954

— *The War at Sea, 1939–1945, vol. II – The Period of Balance*, Naval and Military Press, 2004

—— *Churchill and the Admirals*, Pen and Sword, 2004

Eberhard Rössler, *The U-boat: The Evolution and Technical History of German Submarines, Arms and Armour,* 1981

Floyd W. Rudmin, *Bordering on Aggression: Evidence of U.S. Military Preparations Against Canada*, Voyageur Publishing, 1993

Friedrich Ruge, *The Soviets as Naval Opponents, 1941–1945*, Naval Institute Press, 1979

Markku Ruotsila, *Churchill and Finland: A study in anticommunism and geopolitics*, Routledge, 2005

James Rusbridger, *Who Sank the* Surcouf? *The Truth about the Disappearance of the Pride of the French Navy*, Century, 1991

Robert E. Sherwood, *The White House Papers of Harry L. Hopkins, vol.1, September 1939–January 1942*, Eyre and Spottiswoode, 1948.

William L. Shirer, *The Rise and Fall of the Third Reich*, Simon and Schuster, 1959

Gerald Shone, *U-boat in New Zealand Waters*, Pahiatua Publications, 2016

Jak P. Mallmann Showell, *U-boats Under the Swastika*, Ian Allan, 1973

    —— *Hitler's U-boat Bases*, Sutton Publishing, 2002

    —— *The German Navy Handbook 1939–1945*, Sutton Publishing, 1999

    —— *German Naval Codebreakers*, Naval Institute Press, 2003

Joseph P. Slavic, *The Cruiser of the German Raider Atlantis*, Naval Institute Press, 2003

Sir John Slessor, *The Central Blue: Recollections and Reflections*, Cassell, 1956

Kevin Smith, *Conflict Over Convoys: Anglo-American Logistics Diplomacy in the Second World War*, Cambridge University Press, 2002

Peter C. Smith, *Arctic Victory: Story of Convoy PQ18*, New English Library, 1977

Edward Spears, *Assignment to Catastrophe, Volume 1: Prelude to Dunkirk July 1939–May 1940*, Heinemann, 1954

Tony Spooner, *Supreme Gallantry: Malta's Role in the Allied Victory, 1939–1945*, John Murray, 1996

Robert C. Stern, *Battle Beneath the Waves: The U-boat War*, Arms and Armour, 1979

David Stevens, *U-Boat Far from Home*, Allen and Unwin, 1997

Vaino Tanner, *The Winter War: Finland against Russia 1939–1940*, Stanford University Press, 1956

Julian Thompson, *Dunkirk: Retreat to Victory*, Arcade, 2008

L.C.F. Turner, H.R. Gordon-Cumming and J. Betzler, *War in the Southern Oceans 1939–1945*, Oxford University Press, 1961

Dan van der Vat, *The Atlantic Campaign: Great Struggle at Sea*, Birlinn, 2001

Philip Vella, *Malta: Blitzed But Not Defeated*, Progress Press, 1997

C.E.T. Warren and James Benson, *Above Us the Waves: The Story of Midget Submarines and Human Torpedoes*, Harrap, 1953

Bruce Watson, *Atlantic Convoys and Nazi Raiders*, Praeger, 2006

Herbert Werner, *Iron Coffins*, Arthur Baker, 1969

Ronald Wheatley, *Operation Sea Lion*, Clarendon, 1958

David Fairbank White, *Bitter Ocean: The Dramatic Story of the Battle of the Atlantic 1939–1945*, Headline, 2006

Gordon Williamson, *German Pocket Battleships 1939–1945*, Osprey Publishing, 2003
— *U-boat Bases and Bunkers 1941–1945*, Osprey, 2003

Godfrey Winn, *PQ17: The Story of a Ship*, Universal Book Club, 1948

Richard Woodman, *Arctic Convoys 1941–1945*, Pen and Sword, 1993
— *The Real Cruel Sea: The Merchant Navy in the Battle of the Atlantic, 1939–1943*, Pen and Sword, 2011

Norman E. Youngblood, *The Development of Mine Warfare: A Most Murderous and Barbarous Conduct*, Praeger, 2006

PICTURE CREDITS

Getty Images: 8, 22, 28, 41, 47, 49, 56, 84, 98, 120, 147, 159, 164, 168, 173, 177, 190, 195, 231, 237

Shutterstock: 14, 16, 77, 87, 104, 240

King's College, Cambridge: 90

INDEX